The Art of Looking Back

ALSO BY THERESA KISHKAN

Poetry

Arranging the Gallery
Ikons of the Hunt
Black Cup

Novels and Novellas

Inishbream
Sisters of Grass
A Man in a Distant Field
The Age of Water Lilies
Winter Wren
Patrin
The Weight of the Heart

Essays and Memoir

Red Laredo Boots
Phantom Limb
Mnemonic: A Book of Trees
Euclid's Orchard
Blue Portugal and Other Essays

Chapbooks

Premonitions and Gifts
I Thought I Could See Africa
Morning Glory
month of wild berries picking
Museum of the Multitude Village

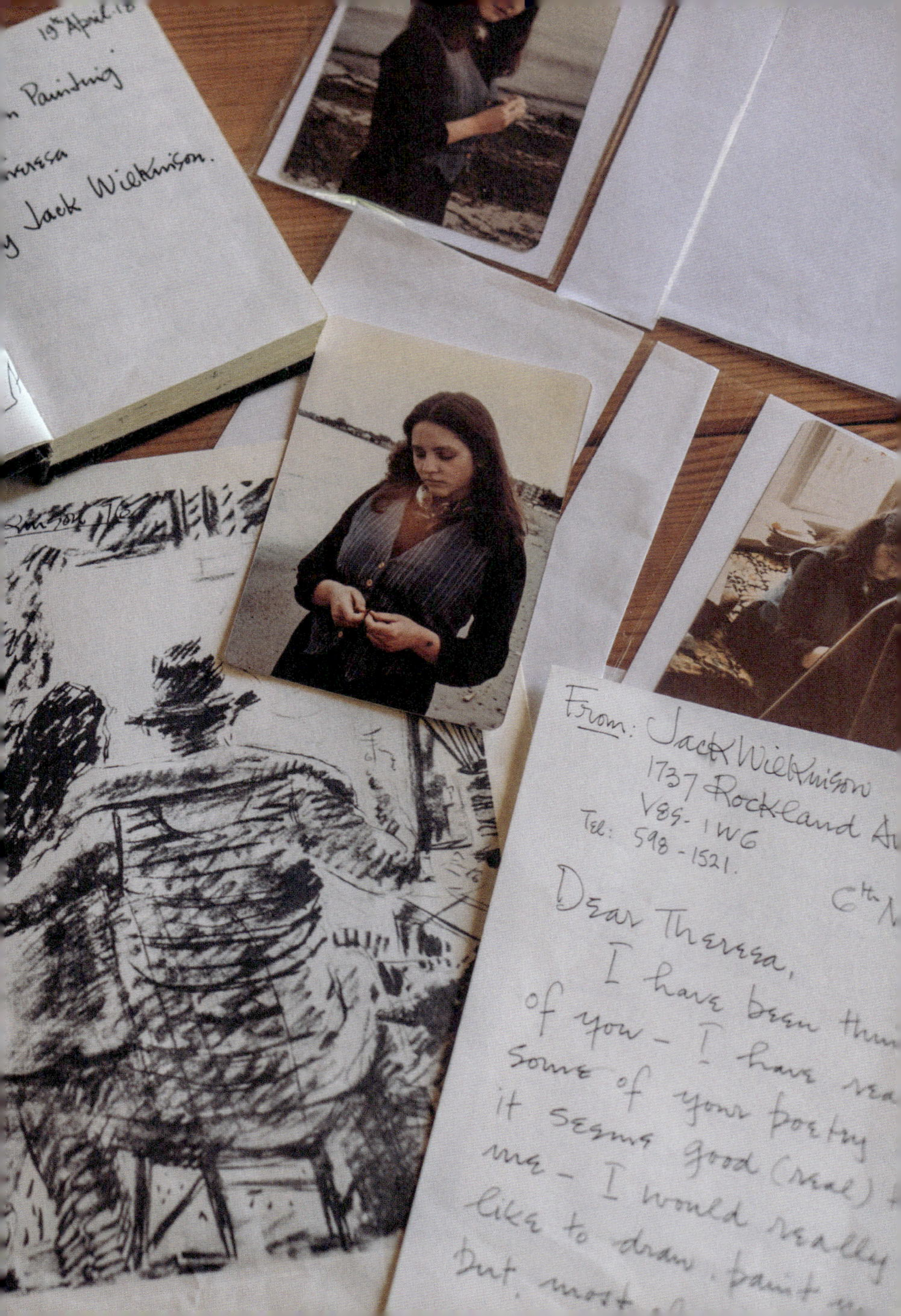

Painting
Jack Wilkinson.
From: Jack Wilkinson
1737 Rockland
V8S-1W6
Tel: 598-1521.
Dear Theresa,
I have been
of you – I have
some of your poetry
it seems good (real)
me – I would really
like to draw, paint

Praise for *The Art of Looking Back*

"Nuanced and poetic, *The Art of Looking Back* details the evolving understanding of a mature woman looking at the tapestry of feelings and experiences from her younger years, especially triggered by memories of a well-known older man's obsessive enchantment with her as a flowering young woman through to her middle years.

Filled with rich reminiscences from earlier years and critical questions posed as an older woman, Theresa Kishkan's poetic and vibrant writing grapples with youth's evolving self-image, the reactions and decisions creating life's trail, and the questions and insight that age can bestow."
—Christina Johnson-Dean, writer, teacher and art historian

"This ground-breaking book examines concepts of shame and complicity and obsession, and so it is, by turns, disturbing, heart-breaking, and infuriating. But most of all it is relentlessly honest and beautifully written."
—Caroline Woodward, author of *Light Years: Memoir of a Modern Lighthouse Keeper* and other titles

"Theresa Kishkan travels an odyssey of her own memories and a lifetime of reflections to recover her younger self from an avaricious, obsessive older man and a society all too eager to judge or look away. By translating the passage of time and knowledge earned along the way into new memories, Kishkan brings the reader on her quest for reclamation. Have our cultural times changed enough to meet the author's gaze?"
—India Rael Young, curator of art and photography at the Royal British Columbia Museum

"Theresa Kishkan's *The Art of Looking Back* excavates art, memory and the boundaries we cross—willingly or not. She recalls her late-1970s style—a faded jean jacket, flowers in her hair, a green hat, or was it red?—while confronting the lingering discomfort of being painted nude without consent by an older, married artist, Jack. She also encounters his even more unsettling depiction of his pre-adolescent daughter—a painting she later purchased and brought home. Each glance revives unease: why did she make it her own? Writing back to histories of domination, Kishkan joins muses and models like Fernande Olivier and Elsa von Freytag-Loringhoven, reclaiming the gaze. Unflinching and vividly rendered, this memoir probes complicity and betrayal, showing art's power to bear witness—and to expose the perpetrator—decades later."

—Irene Gammel, director of the Modern Literature and Culture Research Centre, Toronto Metropolitan University

"*The Art of Looking Back* is a powerful, heartwrenching examination of discovering the complexity of power imbalances, sometimes long after the fact. An artist's muse steps out from the frame that the artist created for her and into her own agency in this beautiful memoir exploring the ripple effects of the male gaze in the world of art."

—Kitty Stryker, author and consent educator

The Art of Looking Back

A painter, an obsession, and reclaiming the gaze

THERESA KISHKAN

THORNAPPLE PRESS

The Art of Looking Back
A painter, an obsession, and reclaiming the gaze

Thornapple Press
300 – 722 Cormorant Street
Victoria, BC V8W 1P8
Canada
press@thornapplepress.ca
Our business offices are located on the traditional, ancestral and unceded territories of the lək̓ʷəŋən and W̱SÁNEĆ peoples. We return a percentage of company profits to the original stewards of this land through South Island Reciprocity Trust.
Thornapple Press is a brand of Talk Science to Me Communications Inc. Talk Science is a WBE Canada Certified Women Business Enterprise, a CGLCC Certified 2SLGBTQI+-owned business, and a Certified Living Wage Employer.

Cover design by DSGN DEPT.
Interior design by Jeff Werner
Substantive editing by Andrea Zanin
Copy-editing by Heather van der Hoop
Proofreading by Alison Whyte

Library and Archives Canada Cataloguing in Publication
Title: The art of looking back : a painter, an obsession, and reclaiming the gaze / Theresa Kishkan.
Names: Kishkan, Theresa, author
Description: Includes bibliographical references.
Identifiers:
Canadiana (print) 20250292874 |
Canadiana (ebook) 20250292882 |
ISBN 9781997702061 (hardcover) |
ISBN 9781997702078 (softcover) |
ISBN 9781997702085 (EPUB) |
ISBN 9781997702092 (PDF)
Subjects: LCSH: Kishkan, Theresa. | LCSH: Wilkinson, Jack, 1927-2007. | LCSH: Artists' models—Biography. | CSH: Authors, Canadian (English)—20th century—Biography. | LCSH: Man-woman relationships—Psychological aspects. | LCSH: Women in art. | LCGFT: Autobiographies.
Classification: LCC PS8571.I75 Z46 2026 | DDC C813/.54—dc23

10 9 8 7 6 5 4 3 2 1

Typeset in Minion and Caslon.
Printed and bound in Shenzhen, China by Reliance Printing.

For Anne Carr, with appreciation for your constant friendship and wise counsel.

Let a body venture at last out of its shelter, take a chance with meaning under a veil of words.

Julia Kristeva, "Stabat Mater"

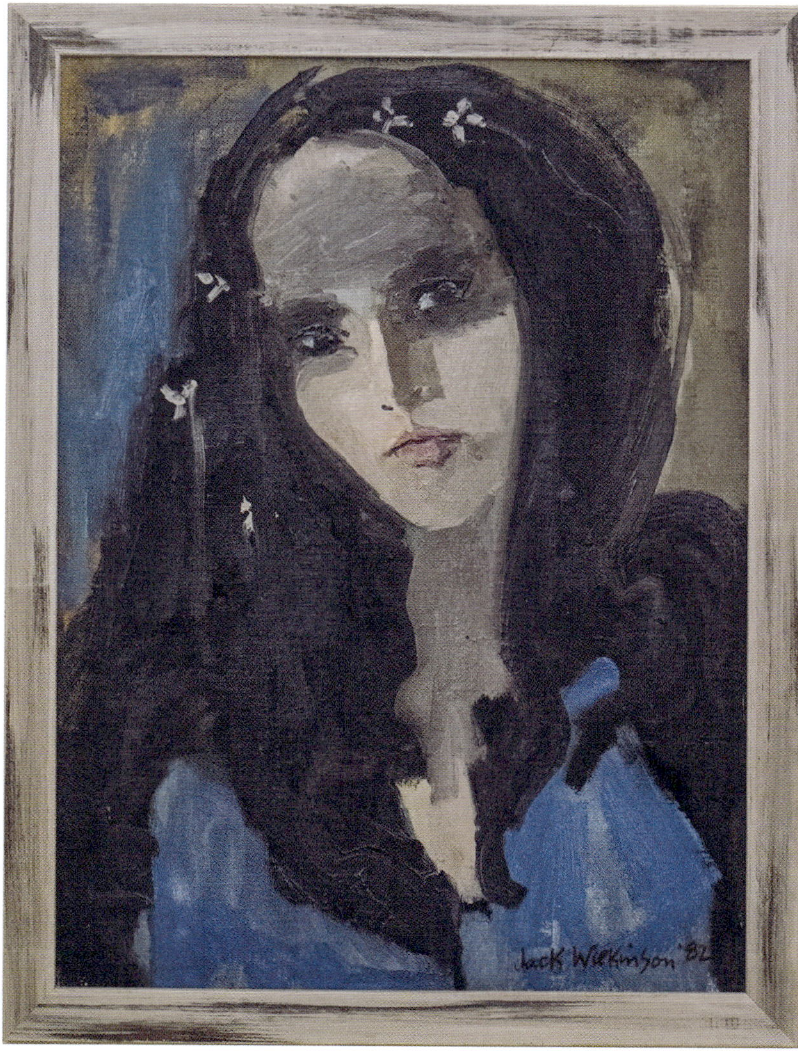
Jack Wilkinson '82

"Meet the painter"

Every morning I descend the stairs from my bedroom and there she is: me, at twenty-three. She has dark hair, strewn with flowers. She is wearing a blue woollen waistcoat with wooden buttons, the one I sewed from fabric bought at Capital Iron. Even if you didn't know me then, you'd suspect I was a poet.

I remember the mornings I'd begin the descent to the kitchen and stop after two stairs, sitting heavily in front of the portrait, too tired to proceed. In those years, with three small children, I was always tired. I didn't sleep well and often I'd lie awake for hours, thinking about the day ahead, the days past. I thought a lot about the painter who brought the portrait as a gift to my daughter when she was born. I remembered vividly the first time we met.

There was a gallery on East Saanich Road, off McTavish Road, Utley's Gallery, and I'd been invited to an opening of a Limners exhibition. The Limners were a group of Victoria artists, brought together in the 1960s with shared interests and aspirations; some of them were close friends, working in collaboration. I knew a couple of the artists through my friendship with Robin and Sylvia Skelton. The Skeltons hosted parties at their big house on Victoria Avenue and I remember a few of the Limners in regular attendance.

For the Utley's opening, I asked a friend if he'd like to join me for the evening and we drove farther out the peninsula for the reception. I wore my black skirt with peacocks appliquéd around the hem, a black leotard, and my brother's faded Levi's jacket. I was finishing my degree at the University of Victoria and I was planning to travel to Ireland once classes finished.

When we entered the gallery, a ramshackle building with rooms on two levels, the first person I encountered was Sylvia Skelton. She took my hand and said, "You must come and see your portrait!" My portrait? No Limner had painted me, not that I knew of, but Sylvia had my hand and was leading me down some stairs to a room hung with many paintings and drawings by Myfanwy Pavelic of an elegant young woman, long-limbed, both naked and clothed; I knew *that* wasn't me. For a time I'd lived on Ardmore Drive, sharing a friend's family summer home, and at night we'd walk by Myfanwy's studio, lit up, and we knew she was working. Tall trees surrounded her house and studio, making things even darker; the glow from her windows in the night sky was entrancing. An artist at work! Maybe she was working on these, which were beautiful. (Her iconic portrait of Pierre Trudeau was still in the future.) "There," said Sylvia, "there you are." And on the wall was a small painting of a girl in a hat. In my memory the hat was green. Or maybe it was red. It wasn't me and yet it was, in a way; it was my head, my hair, my face. Someone gave me a glass of wine and I stood close to the painting, looking at it in wonder. "Meet the painter," Sylvia was saying, and I turned to see Jack.

I turned to see Jack. I turn now to see Jack in almost every room of my house. Others might note his paintings on the walls, but I see his eyes, fierce in their observation. I see his grey hair smoothed back, his beard, his sturdy build. I am looking out from the canvas, the paper, the places where he drew me, painted me, and I see him taking me in.

Was I taken in? I was.

"As you might deduce, I am enchanted"

> But the woman took off the great lid of the jar with her hands and scattered all these and her thought caused sorrow and mischief to men. Only Hope remained there in an unbreakable home within under the rim of the great jar, and did not fly out at the door...[1]

A few days after the opening at Utley's Gallery, an envelope arrived in the mailbox at my parents' house, where I was living while waiting to graduate and leave for the west of Ireland. My parents were away for a month. I'd invited a friend to dinner and she brought her boyfriend, who didn't much like me. To be honest? I didn't much like him either.

Sheryl had been my closest friend since my second year of university. We shared a love of poetry and wild places, discussing our reading, exploring the remote beaches and forests of the lower Island. When she met Michael, our relationship faltered. They seemed to want a settled life of dinner parties, and Sheryl moved from the old house in James Bay where she had a room to the beautiful apartment she would share with Michael. I wasn't invited to their parties because I'd behaved badly in a way that still causes me embarrassment when I remember it from this great distance of years—I will revisit this point later—and the outfall made me a pariah with a circle of people they were eager to be part of. I'd alienated a couple Sheryl and Michael wanted to include in that circle and it was easier to leave me out.

But in the meantime, Sheryl and Michael were at my parents' house when I brought in the day's mail, including an envelope addressed to me in a firm, intriguing script. I didn't even think twice. I opened it in their company. It contained a drawing of a naked woman, her hair long and loose on her shoulders, sitting partly on an artist's knee, both backs to the viewer, looking at a canvas, with Jack's signature in one corner, the same broad scrawl he used to write my name and address on the envelope. There was also a letter, three pages, telling me he'd been thinking of me, had been reading my poems (I'd published a collection of them in 1976), and asking me to get in touch when I could because he wanted to draw me.

> It would be indulgent of me to write
> you a long letter (although I have many
> thoughts I would like to share with you)
> so until I hear from you, I will refrain

> from doing so. Friday night became special for me because I met you. As you might deduce, I am enchanted. (March 6, 1978)

I could tell Sheryl was surprised, at least at first. Michael, too. But then, *not* surprised, not really. I was learning that people understood I attracted older men, not the young guys I wanted to date, but men the ages of their fathers. Maybe my friends thought I did it on purpose. Maybe I had a trick or two up my sleeve. Men at the Skeltons' parties—the artists, the retired booksellers, poets of a certain age. Sometimes I noticed their attentions, yes, but mostly I didn't, though I remember someone else would occasionally tell me about them, pointedly. I'd been a homely girl in grade school, awkward, a reader. When I grew into what I suppose I must call my beauty, I barely noticed because it wasn't the beauty celebrated in the culture of my peers: long slim bodies in bikinis, blonde hair, modest breasts. Those were not my physical characteristics, so it took a few occasions when I realized I was being noticed: the shift from wallflower to attractive young woman. And suddenly, as we looked at the drawing of the naked girl on the artist's lap, Sheryl and Michael had opinions on this particular situation, which also provided a way to voice a collective opinion, not limited to what was contained in the envelope in my hand. The waters were suddenly dangerous and I was out of my depth. Later, another friend, Meg, offered her opinion too. She knew someone who knew someone who knew someone who knew the painter. He's married, she reminded me. He's a father of three. I've heard rumours associated with him, something to do with his young daughter, she said, so it's not surprising he'd be attracted to you. What will you do? They expected the worst of me, or at least the unpredictable. I was learning that. Or maybe I was the risky spark, bright enough for the three of us, young women finding their way in the world.

If my parents had been home, I might have left well enough alone, to use an expression I had heard from my mother so many times in my life. I might have kept my head low. I might have finished my coursework, written my exams and packed my bag for Ireland—and nothing else. Instead, while I did those things, I also got in touch with him. Not right away, but a few nights later, after a drink or two with Meg. Call him, she suggested. If I took the risk, no one else would have to.

"Could you come now?" he asked. "I have been trying to draw your face." It was evening, it was difficult to read the numbers on the houses because of darkness and rain, but it turned out his was the big Maclure house at that turn in the road in the Rockland neighbourhood. Meg came with me. He answered the door and there was that fierce look. No one had looked at me quite that way before. He invited us in, introduced us to his family. He took us into his studio to show us his work. On the drive to his house, Meg, who was tall and slim, had confessed to me that she wanted him to paint her. I was the impetuous wild one in the story she and Sheryl told themselves and later their boyfriends, but it seemed she wanted to take her clothes off and lie on the flowered divan and have him paint her.

I was the one who couldn't be trusted to behave well at the New Year's party, but the previous year, when Sheryl was beginning her involvement with Michael, when he was driving a taxi and coming to her apartment in the wee hours to slip into her bed, he confessed that he was also attracted to Meg. So it was arranged that Michael and Meg would sleep together. Was Sheryl there too? The details were not shared with me, but I remember feeling very uncomfortable in the presence of the three of them for some time. It didn't ever have to be said that Michael wasn't attracted to me. I tell this story now with a new understanding about boundaries.

Jack wanted to see me daily. I couldn't really take the time away from my classes and final papers. But I did see him a few times a week. He drew me obsessively. If I met him for lunch, there would be four drawings at the end of the meal. There was pressure to meet again. Pressure for me to formally model for him. There was urgency. So little time because I was going away.

Look at yourself in the blue vest

Step back. Step back. Look at each portrait of the young woman you were. You were full-bodied. Your friends urged you to lose weight, take more care with your appearance. But in these portraits you see a beautiful young woman, her shape lovingly limned. There was no need to feel insignificant, even if you didn't have a steady or reliable boyfriend. You were writing poems. You'd published a first book at twenty. You were supported in that work by Robin Skelton, who told you that you were a poet. He had solicited and was editing a second collection of your poems. Sometimes he'd write to you to tell you how much he was enjoying the work. The self you saw reflected in his eyes, in Jack's eyes, was not the self your friends saw.

Sheryl and Meg had graduated the year before me and I don't believe they continued to write, or at least not seriously. They no longer brought poems to our meetings for coffee or drinks, no longer talked about ideas for sequences or brief lyrics. I don't remember if they minded, though both of them had written interesting poems. There are lines I remember to this day. I do know I felt that I needed to write regularly; it was bedrock to who I was, the thing I did that made me feel I was alive in all my senses. My true calling. I didn't have a job at that point, or not much of one. Was that the year I worked in the library for eight hours a week? Sometimes small editing contracts came my way. I once cleaned an apartment for $50 and was asked by the building manager if I'd like her to put in a word for me with a friend who was a housekeeper at the Empress Hotel. I declined because I was going to Ireland. I sold my car to pay for my ticket and I was waiting for my income tax return. If things became desperate (and they did), I had someone who wanted to buy the Walter J. Phillips woodcut I'd purchased once on a whim, "Mary at the Lake," because I'd had a small cash surplus as a result of receiving unexpected scholarships, and I was never good about planning for the future. Or maybe I was, because I sold it for four times what I'd paid for it two years earlier. And now when I look at the image online, I see not only its current value, but also how beautiful it is, and how I wish I'd been able to keep it.

Step back. Look at yourself in the blue vest, your face a little thinner than you remember it, the simple white flowers in your hair, your eyes deep and not quite meeting the eye of the viewer. The viewer is also you, forty-four years later. You are wearing the black Viyella shirt you bought in London after you received your father's call to tell you your mother had been diagnosed with breast cancer and you changed your ticket to fly home to help her; you had a little money you'd saved for more travel so you went into a fancy shop in Knightsbridge on your last day in London to buy your mother a grey-blue shirt, soft as fog, and the black one for yourself. You weren't ever good at saving for a rainy day. (Remembering this, you are wearing your shabby red dressing gown, seated on the third stair from the bottom.)

It was a rainy evening when you first visited Jack at his house, you and Meg standing on the doorstep, your dark hair spangled with raindrops, Meg's thin and straight around her face. You could paint me, she suggested in a little-girl voice. He chuckled.

(That first ardent letter, accompanying the drawing. Sheryl and her boyfriend saw me open it, maybe I read the letter to them, I don't remember, but mark this moment, remember it, because of something that happened later.)

Was I passive under his gaze?

Coming downstairs in the morning now, at sixty-seven, I am older than Jack was when we went to Witty's Lagoon with a picnic. I was wearing the black Viyella shirt and the homemade blue waistcoat, and we sat on big logs in the sun and talked of painters, of vision, of art. I was reading Michael Holroyd's biography of the Welsh painter Augustus John. There was a copy of John's portrait of Yeats in the library where I worked and I remembered some drawings I'd seen in London. Quick delineations of faces, his children, his wife Ida with a baby, the lines so pure and true somehow. He had such technique, we both agreed. Who else? Well, Picasso, of course. Jack could talk about him forever. A gallery in Victoria had a small suite of Picasso's drawings, kept in a safe, and he wanted me to see them. "If you like them, I'll buy you one," he promised, but the line I could draw, and would, though not perfectly and without much skill, was between such gifts and me. I loved our conversations and I was flattered by his attention but I was young, I was twenty-three, I felt out of my depth sometimes. I couldn't imagine introducing Jack to my parents, saying, what, "This is the man who bought me the Picasso drawing?" How *could* I introduce them? He was the same age as my father. I knew my father loved me, but never in a million years, or even ten years, would he discuss art with me or consider my opinion on *anything* or tell me I was so beautiful I took his breath away. He didn't really talk to me much at all. Once when I was eleven, he poked my chest and asked, "What's that?" He hadn't paid enough attention to notice I'd developed breasts, and then he did notice. He didn't apologize himself but asked my mother to tell me he was sorry. Anyway, my parents were grudging with compliments. Maybe they didn't see much in me to praise, maybe my mother's Scots Presbyterian upbringing instilled in her the notion that praise was something the devil would notice, so use it sparingly. To sit on a beach in warm sunlight, eating baguette and soft cheese, slices of apple, drinking wine out of small tumblers, while an accomplished man listened to me, argued with me without drowning me out, was a gift (not a Picasso drawing, not money) I couldn't refuse. Even if I knew I should, or at least that was what my friends advised. (I defended Francis Bacon's paintings while he said they were a terrible waste of talent. I thought Gwen John was maybe even a better painter than her brother, Augustus, and he thought that might be true. I'd seen Lucian Freud's work in London the previous year and found it astonishing, though Jack felt it was often cruel to its subjects.)

There was more than a whiff of scandal. Hadn't I noticed, someone asked, that so many of his paintings feature his daughter? Naked? Well, yes, I did begin to see her when I knew to look: paintings leaning against his studio wall, a girl, very young, with beautiful curls, at ease in her full body, so young that she didn't have pubic hair. Astonishing to me, in so many ways. My father didn't look at me enough to notice I had breasts. Until he did: bumps under my T-shirt. I couldn't imagine being naked in front of him.

A few months after that day on the beach, the day I wore my blue vest and a long skirt, he gave me this sketch, a satyr and a full-bodied (and naked) woman sitting together on a log, snuggled together, the woman's hair wind-blown. And I'd thought we were talking about art.

Stop now and look as deeply as you can into the portrait in the stairwell. For years she has made you uncomfortable for reasons you haven't found words for. She was not an innocent in how the body behaves. She'd had a few lovers, even a few she should have known better than to take to her bed. She'd made mistakes. She'd once loved the wrong man, who had never given her any reason for hope that her affection was reciprocal. Maybe more than one wrong man. She judged herself harshly and at that point in her life, she didn't know many people who would let her off the hook of her own self-loathing. (She didn't know she'd forged the hook herself.) She needed to be thinner, something done with her hair, the right man found. The painting hangs from a single hook. When you use a long-handled duster to brush cobwebs from the glass, her face gazes just past you, far-seeing, her eyes shadowed. Sometimes when you dust the painting, you need to straighten it afterwards and you feel woozy, pushing the frame with your duster, your own face behind glass, at a distance, the years refracting, changing direction.

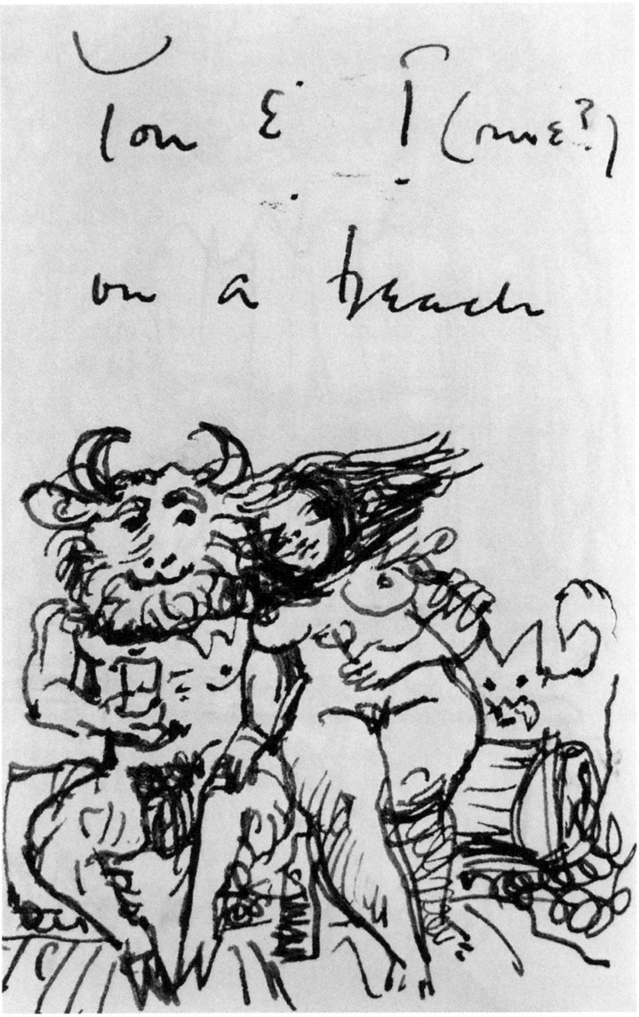

Was I passive under his gaze? I was thinking. Is that passive? He was looking at my body, finding the right colours, perspective, and I was thinking. Or taking myself out of the pose and situating myself in the future, in just a month or two, when I would be travelling to Ireland on my own, to a cottage in the Mayo mountains. I was thinking ahead to the life I would be living after this one, never dreaming they were one and the same. (Never mind that the plan had to be adjusted because the cottage had been vandalized and I found myself on an island off the Connemara coast, about as far from his gaze as I could be, as far from the known world.) I was present in body but not in my mind or my heart.

His wife, Marie, was nice to me. She was elegant, gracious, and welcomed me into her home, or at least that's how I remember it. Yet I must have hurt her, without consciously knowing I could. (I'd have been shocked if anyone told me I had that power.) I admired her. Possibly, probably, she hated me. I didn't have romantic intentions toward her husband. How could I? I was overwhelmed by his attentions but I wasn't attracted to him, didn't want him as a lover. I was flattered. I was interested in talking to him, learning more about art. But beyond that? I don't remember having time to even consider what kind of relationship this was or where it might lead. I wasn't attracted to Jack. I know this is naive but I didn't think romantic interest was a requirement to spend time in his company. And mostly it was good company, at least at the beginning. He thought I might be able to paint and set up an easel for me in his studio so I could try. I made some little watercolours of the village

I'd lived in on Crete. And while I was painting, he was drawing me. Later he gave me a book to take to Ireland, along with a small case of watercolours, a palette, a few brushes and a pad of watercolour paper. The book was advice on composition, on colour, simple suggestions for accommodating light and dark. Or at least that's how it began. But it quickly became a series of drawings of me and notes about his feelings.

Step back again. Ask yourself. Look at yourself in the stairwell and ask yourself. You know the questions. Look at your younger self, try to meet her (your) eye. What did you feel? Was there a time? A time. Be honest. Were you interested in sex with him?

I can truly answer "no."

Once, he kissed me. It was by the trees on his property, near where I parked. He was strong and once I was in his arms, I didn't struggle out of them. He kissed me and I don't remember enjoying it. But he began to shake. If I knew then what I knew a week or two later, I'd have run out the gate and kept on going.

"Where there's smoke"

Two years before I met Jack, in my third year of university, before I took a year off to travel to Europe, I had a stalker. The summer before my third year, I'd gone to a writing workshop in eastern Washington state. I'd been encouraged to do this by the organizer of the workshop, a poet who'd spent the previous term at my university and who'd been very supportive of the poetry I was writing. The workshop was two weeks long and I drove my little Datsun across the state and unloaded everything into the dorm room I'd been assigned for the duration. It was an intense time. I fell in love with a teaching fellow from Arizona, though it didn't work out, the distances between us too difficult to bridge. Most mornings I found myself sharing a breakfast table with the novelist John Williams; he was the star writer at the workshop, leading a workshop for advanced fiction writers. He drank many cups of coffee and he'd always take my cup to fill it too. His manners were courtly. He wanted to know my plans, my dreams, and gave me his address so I could reach him if I needed to. He was teaching at the University of Denver and thought I might like to consider studying there at some point. He could make it possible, he said. At the end of the two weeks, I drove home, a little heartbroken, but also convinced that I would continue to write seriously.

I was living with my parents that year. One afternoon I came home from classes and my mother told me, tersely, that I'd had a phone call from someone whose name she thought was Farmer Peterson. She waited. She expected I'd know who she was talking about. Farmer Peterson? I didn't have a clue. Well, he knows you, she told me. He left a message. He said the photographs were ready.

The photographs? I didn't know what she was talking about. She went on to say that the caller, maybe Farmer Peterson, had told her he was so happy with how they'd turned out. The *nude* photographs, he'd emphasized. He'd taken them in eastern Washington at one of the big parties. She said she'd told him she didn't like how he was talking about me and he assured her that I had a very beautiful body and that the photographs demonstrated it and there was nothing to be ashamed of.

She was so angry at me. How could I have allowed someone to take photographs of me without clothing? I was shocked. I didn't let him, or anyone else! "I don't know who this person is, but it's not true," I told her. She didn't believe me and she made it clear over the next few days that I had disappointed her, disappointed my father, because of course she told him. The two of them were obviously shaken and didn't know how to talk to me about it. They didn't believe me when I tried to tell them that I had no idea what was going on. Disapproval hung in the house like the acrid smoke of their cigarettes, grey and silent.

Over the next two weeks, there were many more phone calls. They were very salacious, the caller describing me in detail—breasts, pubis, buttocks, etc.—and they were always made when I wasn't home. Something dawned. I began to look around at my classmates and others I encountered at the university, people who would know where I was, and when. Only a small number of people knew I'd gone to the writing workshop. And it seemed that one of them was calling my mother to tell her that he had nude photographs of her daughter. He'd tell her that he'd call back when I was home to arrange a meeting to give me the photographs and my mother would pass along these messages, fiercely, angrily, believing what he was telling her about me. She related the details of the calls with a grim expression on her face. Of course I was sorry this was happening to her and it was difficult to remind myself that the messages weren't true.

I didn't sleep those weeks. I had a difficult time concentrating on my work. Someone in my daily life was watching me and calling my home when he knew I wouldn't be there. When I met friends for lunch or found a quiet study carrel in the library to work on papers, was he nearby? Did that person know the details of my drive home? Sometimes I rode my bike. Did he follow me? And finally, after my mother confronted me yet again with a message, I took the phone and called the police. I remember my mother was surprised. And I wonder now why I hadn't done this at the very beginning, but I had no experience that might have prepared me to take action. And no encouragement to take *this* action, because my parents believed I'd done the things the caller said I had.

I remember I talked to a woman police officer and she was very kind. She was reassuring. She told me I didn't need to feel alone. If he called and I talked to him, I was to arrange to meet him, and a team of police officers would meet him instead. But the calls stopped. Maybe I'd told a friend what I'd done—calling the police—and maybe the man who'd been calling had heard, or was told. Now, across the distance of nearly fifty years, I honestly can't know who might have wanted to torment me in this way, and I realize it might have been someone I knew and trusted.

The calls stopped. My parents never apologized for not believing me. If our relationship was built of stones, an arch between generations, they'd removed a crucial stone, the keystone, allowed it to tumble away, undermining everything. Or so it seemed. So when I was seeing Jack the year I was twenty-three, actually taking off my clothes so he could draw me, paint me, I must have felt that it was what they might have expected of me sooner or later. "Where there's smoke, there's fire" was an expression my mother often used. I was beginning to burn.

"Nothing but good"

Nothing prepared me, not my reading, not my modest experience with men, not my own heart, nothing prepared me for the difficulty of his obsessive love, his gaze, and my own reluctance to accept his declarations of need, of hope, of my importance to him. Nothing prepared me.

I found him interesting. I was flattered by his attention. But hearing over and over, reading over and over, what I meant to him and how he knew we were destined to be together, often I felt nervous, listening. If I'm honest, I felt manipulated. I was too inexperienced to firmly decline his affections, though I did decline his physical advances.

> Therefore, I say to you, do not be upset, don't be hurt, nothing but good can come to us by knowing each other dearly. I am sure that you are me, I you, we are of the same tribe. By accident or not, we have passed close to each other. I stretch out my hand, take it, we are meant to, always.[2]

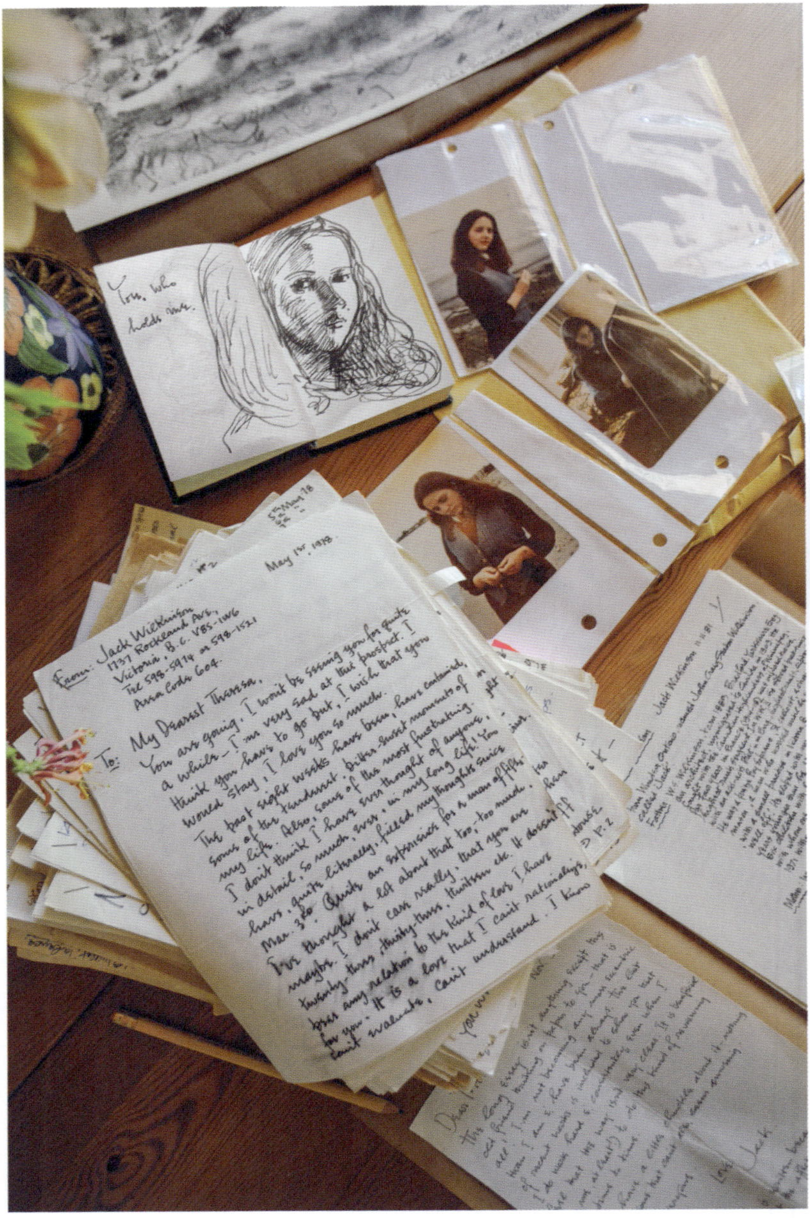

You, who holds me.
May 1st, 1978
From: Jack Wilkinson
1737 Rockland Ave.
Victoria, B.C. V8S-1W6
Tel 598-5974 or 598-1521
Area Code 604
To: My Dearest Theresa,
You are going. I won't be seeing you for quite a while. I'm very sad at the prospect. I think you have to go but, I wish that you would stay, I love you so much.
The past eight weeks have been, have contained, some of the tenderest, bitter-sweet moments of my life. Also, some of the most frustrating. I don't think I have ever thought of anyone, in detail, so much, ever, in my long life! You have, quite literally, filled my thoughts since Mar. 3rd. Quite an experience for a man of fifty. I've thought a lot about that too, too much. maybe. I don't care really, that you are twenty-three, thirty-three, thirteen etc. It doesn't bear any relation to the kind of love I have for you. It is a love that I can't rationalize, can't evaluate, can't understand. I know

The morning of her life

The whiff of scandal. Meg was so insistent that I consider it, because she said everyone knew about it but me. The scandal involved his daughter, Gina, with whom he had a close relationship. Someone Meg worked with knew the family and willingly shared some rumours. They weren't rumours, she insisted, but facts, though the details were murky. His daughter was the subject of hundreds of drawings and paintings. She was five years younger than me. We shared a resemblance. (She was the model for the painting of the girl in the hat, the one that led me to Jack, or him to me. The model that was almost me.) We were both full-figured, dark haired, dark eyed. Her eyes were more almond shaped than mine and her features were more delicate. But we were a type. At that time, we could have been sisters. Almost.

He made a sculpture of his daughter. He said she'd been his dear companion. He painted her naked and clothed, but the beautiful paintings were the former. One, which my husband John and I bought years later, depicts her around age twelve or thirteen, naked, rising from a bed to close the door against the person who has caught her unclothed. The door is slightly ajar and there is an ominous dark knob. (I know, I know.) So there's a troubling element to the painting, but in terms of composition, it is wonderful. And the girl's young skin, her clean bed, the light, oh, the light, the curve of her shoulders as she moves to close the door—it had, *has*, something to say about young girls, power, the ominous dangers that wait for them beyond the safety of their bedrooms. At the threshold. And maybe in their bedrooms, too. Because the hidden subtext of the talk, the matrix of the scandal, was of course a father's obsession with a daughter, their close relationship. *How close* was always the question. At first, I didn't ask this question. It didn't really occur to me, though Meg kept insisting on its possibility. I didn't ask. I pushed the question away.

She is in the morning of her life in that painting. The light is tender and creamy yellow. Later, Jack wrote to me about his daughter's first boyfriend, a young filmmaker, and how he saw them approaching the house one night as the boyfriend walked Gina home. They were holding hands. He said he'd felt cut to the heart. She was lost to him, or at least the close relationship had changed. Was that before we met, or after? I don't remember. The painting hangs at the top of the stairs leading up to my bedroom. I imagine her, a little older than the girl in the painting, in her own room, her own privacy, thinking about the young filmmaker, and rising quickly to push the door shut.

Was that when I began . . . ?

I was shut out of a social group because I made mistakes and I believed then that I deserved to be ostracized. (I still think that.) My worst mistake was leaving a party with a man I admired but who was living with someone else, a woman I also admired. We left the party and he came to my apartment. She followed us and everything fell apart—my friendship with him, whom I'd known first; my friendship with her. People took sides. I took a brief leave from my university classes and I saw a therapist because I was afraid I would hurt myself physically. (I was in terrible pain and I knew I'd caused pain to others.) There was no forgiveness, not for years, but we all eventually found other partners and the wonder is that we all resumed our friendship. But that's years ahead of us and at the time of the event, I was perceived as difficult, even evil. I heard some of the talk and knew by the silence when I entered a room that the subject was a topic of endless discussion among my peers.

Push the door shut on them, those who turned away from you. They can't hurt you now.

(But they did. And they do, though I am decades beyond that time.)

On the evening of the New Year's party at the home of someone I'd considered my best friend, where people I liked and one woman I'd hurt were gathering to eat nice food and celebrate, I sat in my little flat on Oak Bay Avenue and tried to imagine another life. The one I was living felt ruined and sad. Was that when I began to make serious plans to go to Ireland for a year? I think it was.

"I really didn't give a damn what anyone wanted to say about it"

Gina attended a private school in Victoria. One day Jack called me, saying he had to talk to me immediately. Did I drive over? Did we meet halfway? I don't recall. But he was furious because his daughter had been accosted at her school by the janitor, who told her he knew her father painted girls without their clothes, maybe even her. She was very shaken and must have told a teacher or administrator, who told her parents. My name had been mentioned. He wanted to know how the janitor knew me. And I had no idea. Talking to my friend Sheryl later, I told her how upset Jack was and how I was upset too, in turn, to be part of a sordid event at Gina's school. She knew right away what the unknown connection was.

Who the connection was. It was Michael's brother, Rick. The school janitor.

They must have taken the story of my letter, which arrived at my house while they were present. They must have taken the story to Michael's parents' home, where his brother still lived, and it must have been talked about, laughed over, and Michael's brother felt it was something he could use to … well, to what? Make contact with an attractive girl at her school where he was the young man mopping the halls, cleaning the toilets, sweeping the classroom floors? Jack felt betrayed and angry, though not (as far as I knew) at me, or not about that at least, not yet. But at his habits coming to haunt the grounds of his daughter's field? Did that occur to him? And I felt betrayed. I'd become the object of derision in Michael's family home.

> Apparently, he had heard about my "love-letters" from a Michael R., his brother. Anyway, there didn't seem to be much point in pursuing the matter, I really didn't give a damn what anyone wanted to say about it, once I had cooled off. Prior to phoning the janitor I had sought information at the school office & as I was a little worked up at the time, I didn't act very covertly when making my enquiries & involved everyone in the office, including some of the teaching staff & a secretary, who turned out to be Mrs. R, the mother of the "familiar" janitor … No doubt, by the time I was through,

> everyone at Norfolk House was well informed on the Kishkan-Wilkinson affair. (May 5, 1978)

Reading this at the age of sixty-seven, in a house far removed from Victoria, in a life far removed from that one, I feel again the sense of betrayal, *betrayals*, for there are strands, more than one, maybe three, in which I opened a letter in front of two friends, when I should have kept its contents private; in which they shared that information (from *my* letter) with Michael's family (I'd forgotten the detail of his mother working as the school secretary); and in which I was the common element, the strand, that should have been kept private, but wasn't. I didn't ask them to keep it private. I didn't know I needed to.

Reading this letter again, decades later, I realize I was much more complicit in the difficulties within a marriage, a family, even my own resulting—well, what? I hesitate to call it trauma, but is there another term? I don't know one, so I'll leave it blank—than I cared then to acknowledge. I didn't know how to acknowledge my complicity. How did it feel to be Gina, the object of casual mockery by the school janitor? How did it feel to be Marie, witnessing her husband's obsessive ardour directed at a young woman who was flattered but not mature enough to deal with it responsibly? How did it feel for Jack's two sons to witness what must have seemed like a father's foolishness? How did it feel to be me?

In this letter, he is angry at me, though. I was ready to depart for Ireland and he was angry. He wasn't happy at having his attentions refused. I didn't refuse him, but

I took myself away, as I'd planned to for months, ticket bought, typewriter packed. He wrote that "Marie is seeking a 'final solution'. I urge her to be patient. … We have endured an unsatisfactory relationship for a decade too long. … I have made a habit of not expecting anything (until recently)" (May 5, 1978).

There must have been wind

On the beach that day, we could have been a million miles from anywhere. There were birds, the calm water, and there must have been wind because the drawings show my hair in disarray. We'd driven out to Metchosin in Jack's vintage Jaguar. It was made for the winding road, windows open, the scent of the ocean everywhere. Tiny lambs hovered near their mothers in the fields where blue camas was opening to the sun. He said his wife was glad to have him out of her hair for the day. Her dark hair, which she wore in a neat bun, her elegant head on a long neck, her body a ballerina's, which she had been and still was, in a way, teaching children to dance. In the drawings, my hair is wild with wind.

Much later, he wrote to me to say he'd discovered that his wife had been involved with someone else for years, long before I'd met him. Them. Someone close to his family. A member of their extended family: She danced into the future with him. So the complicated braid of betrayals had an unexpected strand. The wide braid gathered in my friends and we were not able to untangle it, but simply to loosen it here or there to allow our own escape. Even now I think of them across the water, the years, and wonder what we'd ever found to say to one another. The evening I'd invited Sheryl and her boyfriend Michael to dinner while I was house-sitting for my parents, I made omelettes with delicate herbs I'd bought at a farm market out on West Saanich Road. Salad. Michael asked for ketchup and salt.

The braid gathered in the ballerina, her lover, and the end of a marriage. It was not my fault. It was entirely my fault.

Stop halfway down the stairs

Stop halfway down the stairs. Why are your eyes so dark, shadowed, slightly averted?

I was not comfortable then with the attention, the painter's gaze. I'm still not.

Look away, look away, look inward. Remember this moment, of all the moments. You are given permanence in pigment, behind glass. A moment, forever happening. The present tense is used to describe things that are happening right now, or things that are continuous.

Behind glass, the present tense of something that happened a long time ago, but is happening every morning when I come down the stairs. The gaze that caught the angle of my face, the blue of my vest, my dark eyes, the gaze that left this earth in 2007 when Jack died but has given me this young woman, myself, her eyes not meeting mine, though I know she sees me in the moment that is now. The gaze has turned, it has turned, what it sees now returns, reciprocates, not lovingly exactly, because in the mornings my seeing isn't as clear as it should be (reading glasses on my bedside table, distance glasses in the car where I need them, the beginnings of cataracts), but with curiosity, a willingness to think about what is appropriated, taken, and what is now given back. For years, the gaze kept me at a distance but some mornings it was a mirror, a threshold.

> Indeed, for imagos—whose veiled faces we analysts see emerge in our daily experience and in the penumbra of symbolic effectiveness—the specular image seems to be the threshold of the visible world, if we take into account the mirrored disposition of the imago of one's own body in hallucinations and dreams, whether it involves one's individual features, or even one's infirmities or object projections; or if we take note of the role of the mirror apparatus in the appearance of doubles, in which psychical realities manifest themselves that are, more-over, heterogeneous.[3]

Though I have a story in which I am on a flowered divan without my clothing

When I entered my sixties, I became invisible, no painterly gaze lingering on the curve of my cheeks, my eyes, my breasts and large thighs. Not that I'd ever been highly visible, as a woman, as a writer. I don't stand out as either, or as other. I am white, heterosexual (mostly), married to my husband for more than forty years, the mother of three children, a grandmother. I've said I'm reserved. I am not exactly an introvert, but I am private. I've published sixteen books, books I'm proud to have written, and they've received some good reviews, are taught in various university courses, but not one of them has been what agents call a breakout book. A book that gets a lucrative deal (because an agent takes it on and finds a good place for it), gets excellent critical attention, film rights, places an author in a more visible position in the writing world as a result. There are books on how to do this, to construct a platform for visibility; courses are taught in the best way to position yourself and your work. I have never been tempted. I've always wanted to find my own way to work with the material I was gathering and when I approached agents for representation, they always wanted something more commercially viable.

I once wrote a novel based loosely on some books of the *Odyssey*, set near my home on the Sechelt Peninsula; the main character, a displaced Irish schoolmaster, was trying to find his way back to himself, and eventually his home, after a terrible trauma, by translating passages of the ancient poem. An agent who read it and agreed to represent me told me, to justify her delay in sending it to publishers, that she'd had a brainwave, that it was her opinion that I could improve my book by making obvious connections between the *Odyssey* and my character's situation on the West Coast of Canada. Draw parallels between the two stories, she said excitedly. I told her all the ways in which those connections or parallels were *already* part of the narrative, how they were implicit in the text, here and here and here, and I wanted them to be discrete and natural. We agreed to disagree and parted ways.

So I was never a bestseller, a chart topper, a household name. And I *was* part of a demographic to which many felt too much attention had already been given. And maybe it had. My ethnicity, my age, my gender, the composition of my household: How could any of this be relevant anymore in a changing world? A changing world, and I was a complex of things I couldn't change. My age, my gender, the person I loved and had married, the quality of my physical and mental health, the children I had given birth to. For years I didn't even name myself a feminist, though I was, in daily practice; I wondered why anyone had to declare one's beliefs, alliances, solidarities to the world at large. I kept them close, not as secrets but simply as my own business, and lived them quietly. I didn't wear trauma on my sleeve or on social media when that became a thing. It was never my party piece. I didn't perform my private life. In short, dear reader, I was—am—dull (though I have a story in which I am on a flowered divan without my clothing and a painter is peering through glasses at my body). Why would we want this person on a panel, at a literary festival, on an editorial board?

There were exceptions. A handful of generous invitations to beautiful places. Wonderful letters from readers, a few really stellar reviews. Of course I kept writing. And increasingly I wanted to think about that gaze, what happened, what it meant and what remains. I want to think about that now, surrounded by paintings, drawings, wondering if they make their own quiet judgment.

Some mornings the glass is not a mirror but a window

> The male glance has often been described. It is commonly said to rest coldly on a woman, measuring, weighing, evaluating, selecting her—in other words, turning her into an object. What is less commonly known is that a woman is not completely defenseless against that glance. If it turns her into an object, then she looks back at the man with the eyes of an object.[4]

When a mostly invisible older woman looks at herself as a young woman, through glass, what does she see? I look. I never realized how small my face seemed within its curtain of dark hair. I felt so exposed in those years, clothed or unclothed. My breasts too large, my calves too wide, my body sturdy. One of the friends from the early years, the tall slim one, used to urge me to lose weight because then I would be "really beautiful" but then "it might be hard to take." What was holding me back? "It might be hard to take." Did that mean our friendship was contingent on my excess weight? My wide hips, my shoulders, my big bum, the fat at the top of my thighs?

"Then she looks back at the man with the eyes of an object."[5]

When I look at myself through glass, I see a girl with flowers in her hair. She is neither fat nor thin. Her eyes are far-seeing; they look inward and outward. She sees me looking at her so far in the future that she cannot imagine the years passing, a husband, three children; the death of first her father, then her mother, dear and close friends (she no longer sees the earlier two), estrangement from others; the building of the very stairs on which I stand, the walls around me, the windows. The gaze that put her down on canvas with rich pigment has given her to me now. Some mornings the glass is not a mirror but a window—into the past, when I was young, troubled, convinced that I was not attractive enough for love. Some mornings I stop, full of awe at my youth, my privacy, even in the public presentation of myself as art.

I am trying to find out who I was, in the light of that gaze, and before it, what foundation held me in place in the whirling years, and how, or if, that foundation became, briefly, a pedestal: "the pedestal isolates the object from the space around it."[6] I was isolated in a certain attention and then isolated in my own pursuit of a body of work that couldn't find a place within the current of time and place.

A picnic on the beach

Was it dishonest to make an image after a day on the beach when I wore a black woolen skirt, a Viyella shirt, the vest commemorated in the image of a young poet with flowers in her hair, was it dishonest to make of that day a little erotic cartoon?

I wonder about Victorine-Louise Meurent, gazing at the viewer in Manet's *Le Déjeuner sur l'herbe,* two fully clothed men on the picnic cloth, another woman draped in cloth and leaning over a little stream, but only Victorine-Louise naked. Her mouth has a slightly humorous turn. Was there a picnic, in the studio or in the woods, and had she removed her clothing? Or is this a liberty taken by Manet? She doesn't seem to be perturbed. She has outlasted the moment. But was it by choice? The basket on its side, her clothing beside it, as though something has happened in a hurry. It's been suggested that the setting for the painting might be the Bois de Boulogne, a popular site for sexual liaisons with prostitutes. What's implied, what's true? I wonder if Victorine has simply come to dry off in the sun after splashing in the stream with her friend. Wonder if the artist wants to suggest she is taking the air after sex. Meaning is as tumbled as the picnic basket on the edge of the frame.

I don't know what sort of reputation Witty's Beach had in those years as a place for trysts, but any other people there that day were beach-walking with dogs or binoculars, stopping to pick up beach glass, enjoying the sun, as I thought we were. Enjoying conversation about art, drinking wine, eating baguette and soft cheese. But clearly Jack had other hopes for the afternoon. Déjeuner, on driftwood. With horns.

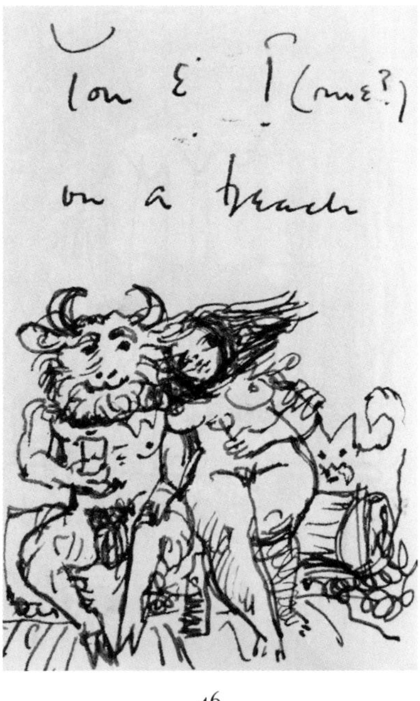

"Let me!"

We had seen each other three times when he wrote this:

> You fill my present, utterly. I want to
> know you—let me! I'll protect & cherish
> you, always. I wish you happiness.[7]

I climbed the hill of the Acropolis in winter

When I met Jack, I was twenty-three. I was preparing to leave for Ireland. Two years earlier, I'd packed the same backpack, red, with outer pockets, a light aluminum frame, two big compartments, and I'd flown to Spain. My intended destination was Greece. I'd hoped that one of my close friends would travel with me but it wasn't going to happen. One friend had no money, another had a boyfriend who didn't like the idea of her travelling away from him, another had parents who disapproved. I decided to go alone and I was both nervous and excited at the prospect. So why Spain, if my desire was to go to Greece? Someone I knew a little, not well, but whom I liked, was going to Spain with her boyfriend around the same time I'd been planning to go to Europe, eventually Greece, on my own. Why not join us for a few weeks in Spain, she suggested, and then take the train to Italy and ferry to Greece? For a young woman raised in Victoria, that sounded exciting. They invited me to dinner in their one-room apartment in an old house in James Bay. We discussed plans and I thought it could work so I bought a ticket for the same flight to Madrid. About a week before the flight, she called to say she'd broken up with her boyfriend ages ago but forgot to tell me. But he was still flying to Madrid, with another girlfriend, and they were OK with me joining them for a brief time.

When we arrived in Madrid, my backpack didn't show up. I was new at world travel and hadn't packed a day bag with a few essentials—toiletries, change of underpants, one fresh T-shirt. The boyfriend spoke Spanish and talked to someone in the airport who was sullen and not helpful. He left the address of the *pensión* where we'd be staying for three nights. I shared a room with the new girlfriend because the owner of the *pensión* didn't want unmarried people in the same bed. It was awkward. They'd arranged travel to the south after the three nights in Madrid and I stayed, hoping against hope my backpack would arrive. Just when I'd decided to simply fly home because I couldn't think of any way to continue, there was a knock at the door and someone shoved my backpack into my room. It was dirty and the canisters of film I'd packed in an outside pouch were missing. But I was relieved beyond words. (In any case, there was no one to say the words to; the words I knew weren't Spanish, the language the *pensión* owner spoke.) I bought a ticket for Italy for the next evening. I had to leave the *pensión* in the morning, after breakfast, and I remember I tried to visit the Prado but wasn't allowed inside with my backpack and I had nowhere to leave it. I sat on its steps, writing in my journal, and watched impossibly beautiful women walk by me in high heels over cobbles, their grace taking my breath away. Twice I was asked to move along by security men with submachine guns looped over their shoulders, so I found other steps leading to a church, and then a bench under some orange trees. A stop in Barcelona where I walked to a museum of modern art and spent a few hours making notes that embarrass me now with their earnest diligence. Then twenty-five hours across France, passing red-tiled villages at dusk, umbrella pines on rocky cliffs, fields of lavender near Grasse, and into Italy.

In Rome I bought a ticket to Brindisi. I asked for a couchette and was assured I would have one, but it turned out I didn't even have a seat. I spent the night in the aisle, leaning against my pack, entertained by a joyous group of Greeks from Manchester. They were heading home to Athens for a wedding. They shared brandy and salty cheese in rolls, for which they handed money out the train window when it stopped, the vendor passing back a paper bag in exchange. After the long meal in Brindisi with the Greeks, who pulled instruments out of their duffle bags in the bar near the ferry terminal and ordered bottle after bottle of rough wine, after the ferry across the Adriatic where the stars came out one by one in a mythic sky, after Corinth, I was in Piraeus, buying a ticket to Crete.

I have written elsewhere[8] of my months on Crete, in a small village on the south coast, and how I loved Agamemnon, helping in his restaurant, swimming most days, walking up the hill behind my room in a house owned by Aphrodite, sitting on rocks surrounded by thyme and rosemary, drinking golden retsina as the sun went down. But after that, I went to Athens and that is what I want to write about here.

I found a room in a guest house in the shadow of the Acropolis. I shared the room with others in the way of those years where you paid for a bed but not privacy. Maybe you had a bunkbed. There was a toilet and you paid extra for a shower; someone would turn on the immersion heater so the water would be warm. In the mornings, breakfast was on a rooftop, wooden chairs around a long table, with warm bread, salty cheese, hardboiled eggs and oranges. Coffee was extra. It came in tiny cups with too much sugar unless you said, "Chorís záchari."

Greece, and particularly the Acropolis, had become increasingly and vitally important to me as a very young woman. I took courses in Classical Greek literature and dreamed of those ancient temples, those skies. I read Plato, the playwrights, Hesiod, the Pre-Socratic philosophers. I read the *Odyssey* in Robert Fitzgerald's thrilling translation, the stories unfolding like my wildest dreams. Greece would be nothing like home, I suspected, and I wanted to travel far from the small house where my parents lived, their opinions and objections not mine. Not mine, though this caused me some anguish. "Isn't home good enough for you?" my father would mutter as I made plans to travel. How could I reply? Later, reading Freud's own late recollections of his experiences in Athens as a younger man, I felt deep recognition. He too had travelled far from his father's expectations of him.

> It is not true that in my school days I ever doubted the real existence of Athens. I only doubted whether I should ever see Athens. It seemed to me beyond the realms of possibility that I should travel so far—that I should "go such a long way." This was linked up with the limitations and poverty of our conditions of life. My longing to travel was also no doubt the expression of a wish to escape from that pressure, like the force which drives so many adolescent children to run away from home. I had long seen clearly that a great part of the pleasure of travel lies in the fulfillment of these early wishes, that it is rooted in dissatisfaction with home and family.[9]

I climbed the hill of the Acropolis in winter, a hill I never expected to climb, my family forgotten. I knew exactly how to find it because the hill was illuminated after dark and I could see it that first night from the rooftop of the guest house. The marble steps were slippery under the sandals I'd bought in an Iraklion street market. Dry stalks of summer plants fringed the path—wild oats, henbane, the desiccated leaves of coreopsis. A few seedpods from spring's poppies. At the bottom of the hill, cypresses, pines and olives, with the prickly leaves of acanthus under their shade. Did I pay? I must have, though I don't remember. But I do remember the Odeon of Herodes Atticus just off the path, the five gateways to the Propylaia, the temple of Athena Nike, the Parthenon (of course) with bereted men taking photographs of tourists highlighted against it. What I remember best and most was the Erechtheion complex—the temple of Athena Polias, the Tomb of King Erechtheus, and the porch of the Karyatids or Kore. There were originally six of the Karyatids, though one was removed by Lord Elgin in the first decade of the nineteenth century and sold to the British Museum; a replica of the lost sister stood in her place when I was there. In 1978, the remaining five maidens were removed to the nearby Acropolis Museum and replicas installed in their places. But in 1976, they stood in their original beauty, holding up the entablature of the porch on the south side of the temple, and for me they became profound emblems of strength. Their bodies were foundational, structural; they were not the objects of anyone's gaze, or if they were or had been, it was immaterial after 2,500 years. Their own eyes were far-seeing. Their clothing closely fit their strong bodies, one leg taking the burden of the building's weight, that leg bent forward to demonstrate their strength. From behind, I could see the intricate braiding of their long hair, thick and bold, serving to enforce the strength of their necks as they supported the burden of the entablature.

It was cold in Athens. I wore a sweater a woman in the village on Crete knitted for me with wool from the village sheep, and warm brown corduroy pants. But when I saw the Karyatids in their elegant draped himations, each with a peplos pinned at the shoulder, blousing over the zone or girdle at the waist, when I saw the long vertical lines of their garment hanging like a veil, I wished for a more comely wardrobe for myself.

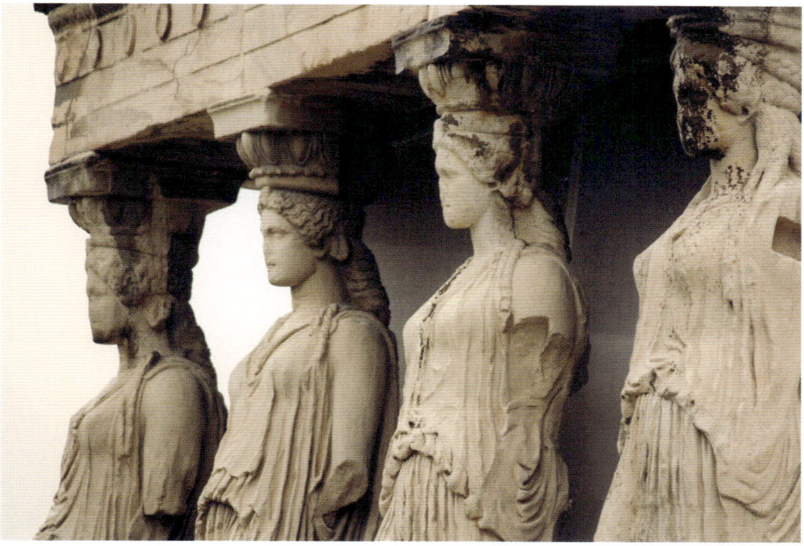

Who created these maidens? No one is certain. The architect of the Erechtheion was the Athenian Mnesikles and the workshop of Phidias is credited with some of the significant sculptures on the Acropolis, notably the Athena Parthenos inside the Parthenon itself. Maybe Alkamenis, or maybe Kallimachos, who was known for his draperies clinging to the bodies of his sculptures, created these Kore. I don't think it was Phidias, though. I don't see his style in the bodies of the six maidens. Each one is different, each face distinctive. They have been damaged and repaired: Kore D was hit by cannon-fire in 1826 and her head was detached. She was mended in 1837. Kore F was found in fragments in 1837 and mended in 1846; part of her head was missing, as was her neck, her arms below the shoulders, her pelvis and her thighs. An Italian sculptor repaired her. No matter. They have lasted more than 2,500 years, and they have entered our consciousness, our lexicon of beauty. They were carved out of Pentelic marble, from the north slope of Mt. Pentelicus, northeast of Athens, a beautiful white marble that glows golden in sunlight. (Phidias preferred bronze or else chryselephantine, in which the flesh of a statue was carved from ivory and the draperies were gold.)

More than 2,500 years later, when I was a young woman, no one wanted to be muscular. The cover girls on the fashion magazines were reed thin, angular, with small pouty breasts. One of my two good friends was tall and slim; the other was my height but perhaps thirty pounds lighter. I walked long distances. I rode a bicycle to and from my classes at the university. I was not unfit. My shoulders were broad and strong, a legacy of my Eastern European forebears.

After I travelled through southern Europe, after spending time in Italy in the company of two nurses I met in Greece, after a couple of weeks in the south of France in the home of artists I'd met on Crete, I went to London, where I found a position at a rehabilitation hostel for ex-psychiatric patients. I was paid pocket money and given room and board. In return, I accompanied residents to job interviews, talked to the ones who wanted to talk to me, filled in for the cleaners who were always quitting because there was too much work for too little pay. I'd vacuum stairs, hallways and common areas; wipe the tables in the dining room; clean toilets and polish sinks. The residents were responsible for their own rooms. Once the cook quit for a week and I was asked to take her job until she was coaxed back, the head nurse visiting her daily until she relented and returned. She kept a scribbled list of her meal plans for a typical week and I tried to replicate her Bolognese sauce, her macaroni and cheese casserole, her baked chicken legs with mushroom sauce (the secret was Campbell's soup). The number of people eating these meals varied, but it was never fewer than twenty; sometimes as many as thirty. I made huge sheet cakes dense with raisins, and Bird's custard to have on top. Apple crumble, the sink filling with curls of peel, tinned cream to have over it. The kitchen was mildly horrifying with its decades of grease and grime, the dry rot in its walls, peculiar little insects creeping out from cracks. I filled buckets with cleaner and scrubbed each foul surface. I'd fall into bed each night to sleep the long sleep of a labourer. Which I guess I was. One of the nurses commented on my stamina and it was a little warm fire I carried inside for days. I could do this, even if it wasn't exactly the life I'd imagined for myself. On a warm February morning, I went into the back garden and weeded the overgrown borders where I found snowdrops and crocuses, early daffodils and a few clumps of hellebores, and then set out a few chairs in case anyone wanted to join me for tea. One resident did, a man called Alistair who was devastatingly handsome but also manipulative and (it was whispered) psychotic. I wore so many layers of clothes in that cold hostel that no one could have known if I was muscular or not.

I would like to say that I carried the influence of the Karyatids home with me as an inspiration, a touchstone of strength and selfhood; I can't help but think how much easier my twenties would have been if I'd known to keep them always in mind. I do remember them, though, and have thought of them often since, though not in relation to myself. That dedication to a purpose, in their case, the task of holding up the roof of a temple porch, the temple housing the Palladium (an olive wood effigy of the goddess Pallas Athena). Against one outer wall of the temple, an ancient olive tree, a moria, sacred to Athena. Above the temple, the same blue sky that Sappho saw, and Homer.

"Let a body venture at last out of its shelter"[10]

> What is less commonly known is that a woman is not completely defenseless against that glance. If it turns her into an object, then she looks back at the man with the eyes of an object.[11]

She looks back.

It takes time. Years, decades even: You have been an object, you stand draped in a pale gauzy shawl in someone's house in Victoria, BC, in a red kimono in your own house, on a flowered divan in private and public collections, in charcoal and ink in folios, and what is seen is the clear skin of a young woman with dark hair and large breasts. An object of beauty, of painterly attention, unnamed, unprotected in a cold studio (no sign of goosebumps, though you remember them on your arms the time you took off your clothing).

To be naked is to be without disguise.

To be on display is to have the surface of one's own skin, the hairs of one's own body, turned into a disguise which, in that situation, can never be discarded.[12]

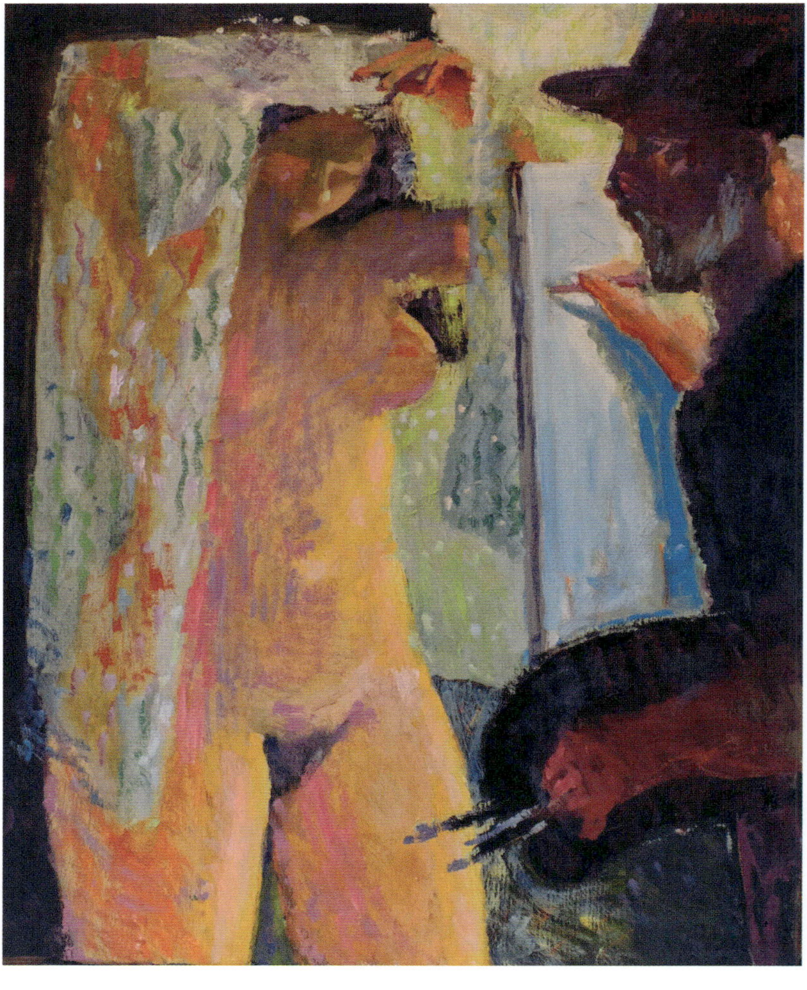

This painting hangs in a room in Victoria, owned by someone I've never met. I was naked and I became a nude. I stood without my clothing, draping a Japanese cloth over my head, while colours were mixed, brushes chosen, and my disguise was my hair, the dark triangle of my pubis and the fall of black hair over my shoulder.

> Let a body venture at last out of its shelter, take a chance with meaning under a veil of words.[13]

You were the object—and now? You are looking back. Stand as close as you can to the image of your younger self, the one in the blue vest. What does she have to tell you? She looks beyond you, eyes averted. But you need to talk to her, to listen to her story. Her story takes decades to tell and it leads right to your door, to your stairs, to the room where you sit on a couch with a cup of coffee or a glass of wine, ready to listen. And ready to take the necessary steps to reach your whole self.

> It is a most painful procedure to tear off those veils, but each step forward in psychological development means just that, the tearing off of a new veil. We are like onions with many skins, and we have to peel ourselves again and again in order to get at the real core.[14]

To peel away the outer skin, to tear away the veil, is to find the creamy-skinned body of a twenty-three-year-old young woman, impulsive, dreamy, occasionally thoughtless. Her face is lit from within, candlelit, soft and glowing. She looks out from under a fall of hair, not really meeting my eyes. Or the painter's eyes. Clothed or unclothed, she is holding something back. Keeping something near. She is hoping her parents don't find out she has taken off her clothing for someone whose intentions are not entirely honourable, though for years afterwards he insisted on his deep love, his care for her well-being, before she entered a marriage with someone else, and after.

> To be naked is to be oneself.
> To be nude is to be seen naked by others and yet not recognized for oneself.[15]

Which was it?

I forgot about Frank

Wait. I forgot about Frank. In my account of my time at the rehabilitation hostel in London, of my work there in the kitchen, halls, bathrooms and garden, I forgot that in my last week, the bookkeeper, a retired Army officer who painted on the side, invited me to lunch. He was quite a nice man, I thought, so I was surprised when Catherine, one of the nurses, the one who handed out little paper cups of pills to residents lined up each morning and evening in a room next to Frank's office, warned me to be careful. I wasn't sure what she meant—I was twenty-one—but kept her words close. At lunch in an intimate French restaurant, over vichyssoise, some delicate fish, other courses I've now forgotten, Frank told me about his life, his war years, his wife whom he'd rescued from somewhere I've now forgotten (like Frank, almost), her nervousness, her fragility. He kept pouring a very good wine. At the end of the meal, he ordered us each a glass of Château d'Yquem. I should have suspected some request would follow, though I didn't, not then. But a request did follow. He confided that he would very much like for me to model for him. It wasn't often, he said, that he met a woman who he felt so strongly drawn to as an artist. Would I allow him to paint me? Flustered, and a little drunk on good wine and sublime Château d'Yquem, a nectar that slid down my throat like a golden serpent, I said I would be willing. Then, almost leering, he professed that what he most hoped was that I would allow him the honour of painting me nude. I didn't know how to say no.

But the sitting never happened. That very evening, my father called to say my mother had been diagnosed with breast cancer and so I arranged to fly home instead of going to Dublin to meet the young women I'd travelled with in Italy, and the next day I couldn't get out of bed. Maybe it was stress and shame and fear. Maybe it was just a hangover from unaccustomed quantities of fine French wine and that treacherous Château d'Yquem, which had taken away my common sense so that I couldn't hear the nurse's warning in my mind, but whatever it was, I was unable to walk, I ached in every bone and muscle, and I had a very high fever. My room was at the front of one of the Victorian houses where the hostel was situated, my bed in its generous bay window. Catherine brought me soup and juice and she was sitting on the edge of my bed when we both heard a tapping on the glass. She pushed aside the curtains and there was Frank, standing in the border below my window, with a sheaf of flowers. "May I bring them to you?" he asked, and Catherine answered for me, opening the window a crack. "She can't see anyone," she told him, "her fever is sky-high and she's just had terrible family news, but if you leave the flowers on my desk, I'll put them in water and bring them to her room."

There was no question that I would visit Frank's studio, conveniently not in his home but in a building near the hostel. No question that I would do anything but organize my red backpack, visit the travel agent to cancel one flight and book another, and buy my mother and myself Viyella shirts in Knightsbridge.

I'd forgotten about Frank, but now I wonder what that extraordinary meal had cost him, a man down on his luck, because as Catherine had observed, though not in his presence, "What's a retired army officer in his golden years doing here, working on our accounts for minimum wage, there's a story there." I wonder if the lunch was worth it. Never since have I been offered Château d'Yquem with a wedge of fine blue cheese and tangy baguette, the taste of each one unforgettable, even though I forgot about Frank.

"Your cool little goodbye note"

In many ways Ireland was the best place to go. I'd been put in touch with an elderly woman who I was assured could help me find a place to live. When I wrote to her, Sheila immediately invited me to stay with her while she figured out where to put me. (Those were her words.) The man who'd connected us said she lived in a caravan, a trailer we'd call it, in a field of cattle in the shadow of a round tower in a little village. She attracted stray and wounded animals, he said, and that's why she called her caravan the "Ark." When I arrived at her gate, I was both stray and wounded. For the previous week I'd wandered galleries and museums in London and Dublin, finding image after image of wild landscapes and grieving women. I wasn't grieving but I was troubled, in pain. I regretted the way I'd left a letter tucked in the mailbox on Jack's front porch. He'd call and I wouldn't answer the phone.

I'd learned that he never wanted to take no for an answer. No, I can't drop everything and meet you. No, I can't, I won't, postpone my travel plans. No, I won't. I can't. A coward, I wrote a brief note telling him goodbye. A letter arrived at the Ark soon after I did.

> One hell of a black day, all of it loneliness, sadness & loss, swept into a pile of regret in my system. It wasn't easy, at first, to digest your cool little goodbye note, but after some thought, I convinced myself that you must have had some very good reasons for not coming to say goodbye & collect your drawing which I had taken the trouble to mat. As I write, it still hurts, though. (May 6, 1978)

It hurt me too, to recognize my own willingness to forgo a proper farewell, but I knew it would not go well. To realize I was in deep water, too deep for comfort, the depths filled with murky life I wasn't comfortable knowing about.

On the plane to London, and then on the train to Holy Head, on the boat across the Irish Sea, walking through Dublin's damp ancient streets, sitting in a pub with some musicians I'd met on the bus from Dun Laoghaire into the city centre, I had the fearful regret heavy as a stone in my body. Fearful because I was realizing that Jack wasn't entirely stable and what would I do if he followed me? It felt entirely possible. And regret because I felt responsible for his emotional turmoil. What could I have done differently? I had not been the one to initiate his obsession, his pain, at least not knowingly. But I *had* opened the envelope, released sorrow, disease, vice, violence, greed, madness, old age, death. I'd gone to his house. I hadn't said no, this is not for me. And nothing in my limited experience prepared me for what happened during those weeks after our meeting.

In many ways Turlough was the best place to arrive, its little cluster of buildings, its eleventh-century round tower topped with a conical cap. The caravan was parked at the bottom end of a field. The farmer who owned it left a hose at the top of the field for water, for Sheila and the cattle and the single donkey who lived in the field. Sheila was tiny, in her late seventies, and it was helpful for me to take a pitcher or kettle up to the tap, to empty the bucket she used as a toilet (that I used too), sheltered in a tent, anyway, to empty it along the line of fuchsia and hawthorn growing as a hedge along the stone wall separating the field from the back gardens of the row of houses that was the village. We burned the toilet paper in her little stove, along with bricks of turf and any sticks we found on our walks. Sheila had been an artist and when I told her something of my story, she said immediately, tartly, that of course he had been drawn to me but his feelings were his own business and he shouldn't have burdened me with them. She didn't have a lot of use for men.

I slept on a bench below the window, rolling out my sleeping bag each night and rolling it up again in the morning. There was a dog, Johnny, who'd appeared like me at the gate, wanting refuge and a place for his infected leg to heal; and several cats. Hooded crows flew over daily from the round tower where I think they roosted; their ash grey plumage, punctuated by black head, throat and tail, became familiar in the hedge as they waited for toast scraps. Sheila was a vegan but didn't mind if I had milk on my oatmeal (she took a jam jar up to the farmer and he filled it with creamy milk from one of the cows who rubbed against the caravan). She made omelettes with millet, flavoured with snippings of wild garlic, and she made strong French roast coffee from Bewley's in Dublin in a small brown jug, using a tea strainer to pour it into our cups. I hitchhiked into Castlebar and brought back almonds for her nut milk and cheese for myself. I brought us a bottle of French wine, and oranges. Dark chocolate, vegan approved. She picked St. George's mushrooms and fried them in olive oil.

After a couple of days we went looking for a place for me to live. She'd arranged for me to caretake a cottage up some hills above Foxford, which we got to by bus, taking Johnny, a cottage owned by a forester she knew, but when we got there, we discovered Travellers had camped by it, burning the kitchen and sitting room floorboards for fuel. I didn't need much but I did need a floor. She asked a few people she knew. There was a man in Louisburgh who couldn't offer a house but *did* have an extra table. Someone else wondered about that house over to Parke where everyone had either died of the rheumatism or become too crippled with it to move because it was built right up against a seeping bank, but he didn't know how to get in touch with the owner, who lived in France. Someone else who occasionally brought Sheila ailing animals to care for and who knew everything about everyone couldn't think of anywhere likely. One morning I packed up most of my belongings and headed out to find somewhere, hitchhiking down the west coast, stopping in each small village to ask at the post office if anyone had a rough cottage they'd rent cheaply. A fish dealer in Clifden called one of his suppliers, a fishing family on an island off the coast, and they offered an empty cottage. Which was where I went, after returning to Sheila to pick up the rest of my stuff and to provide a new address for my mail. At her insistence, I went to talk to the farmer about having the donkey's hooves trimmed. They were so long, they curled up at the ends like Arabian slippers. He smiled, sucked away on his pipe, and went on with what he was doing, which was fixing a fence with some lengths of salley.

All this took two weeks. I'd stopped expecting to see Jack at the gate, limping like Johnny or hang-faced like the crows. And by the time I'd moved to the island, where one crossed the passage of water by currach and where my windows faced the sea, where I had no telephone and where no one knew how to find me, where the mail came once a week, also by currach, I'd stopped waiting for the other shoe to drop. Temporarily, that is. Because I still feared he might follow me.

How much of this does the young poet in the stairwell know? It happened after she was painted with the white flowers in her hair, but she looks like she anticipated everything. ("The broken wall, the burning roof and tower / And Agamemnon dead."[16]) When she looks past me, her eyes slightly hooded, is she being evasive or all-knowing, or is she simply bored? Every morning she sees me come down the stairs in my old red bathrobe. Often I am weary because I don't always sleep well. When my children were young, I'd take a minute or two to sit down on a low stair and look at her, my face resting in my hands, my elbows supported by my knees. In those years I barely wrote anything. I told myself (and others) that I wanted to but didn't have the time. In truth, I had as much time for writing as I had for anything else. It wouldn't have mattered if the laundry waited or we ate a simple supper of bread and cheese occasionally. I was filled with love for my family and to be honest, I didn't know what to do with it, apart from folding clean T-shirts and baking loaves of whole-wheat bread, changing the sheets on every bed on Mondays. If I tried to make the love into words, they felt mawkish, unsettling, but baking cinnamon buns to be waiting warm for my children's arrival after school felt like I'd found a way to put my love into action that translated those words into something they could hold in their hands. If I looked up at the poet, her hair dressed in white flowers, I didn't expect her to be of any help. She was waiting for me to acknowledge what had happened, before my husband, before my children, before the flight away from Victoria, my father's blue Optimus stove packed in my red backpack, a fresh notebook in one of the outer pockets.

> Words that are always too distant, too abstract for this underground swarming of seconds, folding in unimaginable spaces. Writing them down is an ordeal of discourse, like love. What is loving, for a woman, the same thing as writing.[17]

"1965–66? I fell 'in love' with my daughter"

"There's more than a whiff of scandal associated with him."

How much of this is my story to tell, and how much of it is the one he was central to, one that rippled out into the world, my singular circle just one of many. How much. I tell what was—*is*—mine. But I was only chosen to be part of the story entire because I resembled his daughter. Because a painting of her in a colourful hat had become a painting of me. In a long essay on his life that he wrote for me (maybe to help me understand his feelings about me, but maybe he was hoping I would write a book about him, a book about his artistic work, and would need ready access to biographical detail, etc.—this was the world before the internet, after all), anyway, in the long essay he wrote:

> 1965–66? I fell "in love" with my daughter. I don't know precisely when it happened, but I have seen works done at that period when it seems that my feelings for her, which eventually became obsessive, were commencing. She was very much my archetype & not only physically, but intellectually. She enchanted me. It lasted until she was nearly eighteen, when her life began to assert itself, a life that had to exclude the father. During the last two years of my thralldom to her, I became very concerned about my sexual attraction to her & painted & made drawings in series, using "the artist & model theme, motif, etc." I have regarded the series as a form of exorcism. Unfortunately for my image, the bigots and pariahs common to any small place, the blunt expression of sensuality was read as incest & I had to learn about the error of being too objective in a public situation (where a majority deals in subjective attitudes). My love for her is intense but not perverse.[18]

Stop halfway down the stairs. Why are my eyes (my eyes, her eyes) so dark, shadowed, slightly averted? She has something to tell you (me). Take a deep breath. Think about this, she whispers. You were a cover, a decoy, or maybe a replacement. It could be as simple and as complicated as that. (Was it?) She is looking at him looking at you. But who is he really seeing?

Turn toward me

He counted the days, the hours, in my company. He knew how many times he'd seen me. Where, how, why.

Turn toward me, I ask the young woman with flowers in her hair. *Face me. We need to talk. In one letter he says he never talked about you to anyone but then he says he asked your publisher about you while he was arranging to have drawings reproduced at the printing offices where the publishing company was located. Some were drawings of you. Your publisher told him everyone was following your romance with a fisherman in Ireland. (You'd only told your two friends in letters, and your editor.) He talked to your editor and your editor's wife, both of them responsible for making a safe haven for you during difficult times so maybe they were relieved you were having a happy romance. (They gave him your mailing address.) He talked about you to the woman who had the bookstore in Oak Bay, the woman you thought never noticed you browsing the shelves or sitting quietly on a chair during a poetry reading, and reported that she'd told him airily, All the men fall in love with her.*

Did you know this? Did you honestly know you had that reputation? Maybe you were beginning to realize that you did attract certain men, like Jack. Like the middle-aged professor of Russian who sent a note to your table, with a glass of cognac, saying he felt you had things in common, though you'd never met him. Like the man who stalked you in your third year of university until you got the police involved. Like the former poet-in-residence who wanted to marry you and take you back to Italy with him but you deduced he was looking for someone to cook for him and manage his papers. You were twenty-one. He was sixty. Turn to me again. You must have known that a particular type of man found you attractive. You didn't try to be a femme fatale. Turn, turn.

To be reminded now, at the age of sixty-seven, having lived a good and productive life with a man I married forty-three years ago, causes my face to heat with shame.

From an article in *Scientific American*, "The Scientific Underpinnings and Impacts of Shame":

> We feel shame when we violate the social norms we believe in. At such moments we feel humiliated, exposed and small and are unable to look another person straight in the eye. We want to sink into the ground and disappear.[19]

I did want to disappear sometimes, into that consoling ground. That's why I wore old denim overalls and work boots (though there was also a velvet-bodiced dress with a skirt printed with bright cherries. It laced over my breasts and made me look like Carmen). I wanted to attend my classes, drink with my friends in the student pub, walk downtown, and be invisible, the way I am now with my worn face and surgical mask. I knew the values my parents held dear were shaken a little by the men that were attracted to their daughter. I didn't tell them anything but I suspect they knew from the phone calls I'd take in their kitchen, declining or accepting invitations that would have shocked them had they known the details. The one invitation in particular, which involved taking off my clothes and lying on a flowered divan in the studio on Rockland Avenue. Even though Jack's wife was in the other room and even though she brought me a cup of tea in case I was chilly. I don't know why I said yes. Maybe I tried to say no but he persisted. Then, and later, there was that pressure current, the conversations and letters that began one way and ended up another. Where there's smoke, there's fire, my mother used to say, and I wonder at the smouldering attentions directed at me. Did they know I could burn so easily? Did I know?

> Shame makes us direct our focus inward
> and view our entire self in a negative light.
> Feelings of guilt, in contrast, result from
> a concrete action for which we accept
> responsibility. Guilt causes us to focus our
> attention on the feelings of others.[20]

Guilt, too, for my part in what happened to the painter's marriage. He assured me it had nothing to do with me and I believe that was ingenuous. I was flattered by his attention at a time in my life when my friends were pairing up and I had no prospects for love. I wasn't attracted to him physically but I was curious about the possibilities of friendships across generations. I told myself that. I was ingenuous too.

“It is only the difference in time zones that hasn’t made possible the joining of our Odysseys”

When Jack wrote about his loves, he called them his archetypes. I wondered about that. Did he mean he carried an ideal image deeply in his consciousness and had moments where a woman somehow answered that image, the questions it might have asked of him? It seemed to me that he wrote and talked about his archetypes, his discovery of a girl or woman whose beauty was correlative to the ideal, but then his behaviour became obsessive, self-destructive. Later, he confessed to me that he was being treated for depression, and I understood that perhaps he was not entirely stable.

I remembered reading Carl Jung's *Memories, Dreams, Reflections* in my early university years and being taken by his work on the relationship between psychosis and a hoard of imagery that he felt formed the matrix of a mythopoetic imagination. I know from my writing life that a hoard of imagery is foundational to my work. I think it was the same for Jack.

> It [that mythopoetic imagination] is something that lives of itself, that makes us live; it is a life behind consciousness that cannot be completely integrated with it, but from which, on the contrary, consciousness arises.[21]

I can believe that he might "recognize" a woman from his internal imagery. But reading "My Life for Theresa Kishkan," a biographical essay Jack wrote for me in 1981, I see a common element in every description of his encounters with his archetypal women. His recognition, his adoration, crosses a line to become what seems to me to be an unhealthy obsession. Is it psychosis? Looking back, I consider the archive I have from that time with Jack. I have this stack of letters, written between 1978 and 1997. Each begins in a very congenial way, responding to letters of mine, to news of my life with my husband and children. But quickly, as the pages accumulate, the assurances that he is my friend, that he would never do anything to harm me, turn to something like an *idée fixe*.

> ... the encounter of a soul mate. That is who you are in my life & knowing you through

> your letters & poems & occasional meetings always tells this. Easy thinking—I mean it in its profound sense. It is only the difference in time zones that hasn't made possible the joining of our Odysseys; I always feel a little cheated by the Fates because there is a sense of belonging that no amount of cynicism ever dispels. (June 30, 1989)

Where am I in this reverie, as a woman, as a person who married a man she fell in love with, had children, made a life for herself in a place she loved? It wasn't only time zones that prevented our "Odysseys" from converging. I'd made choices, after all, and those should have been acknowledged in a meaningful way. But I was the image, the archetype, the object of the gaze, the source of a body of art in this wandering tale, the hero's journey, a story he told to me and others.

All this did exist

> When, finally, on the afternoon after our arrival, I stood on the Acropolis and cast my eyes around upon the landscape, a surprising thought suddenly entered my mind: "So all this really does exist, just as we learnt at school!" To describe the situation more accurately, the person who gave expression to the remark was divided, far more sharply than was usually noticeable, from another person who took cognizance of the remark; and both were astonished, though not by the same thing.[22]

All this did exist. I was a young woman, caught in something I couldn't resolve myself or to anyone else. And now I am astonished to see myself in those years, framed in a stairway, an object of strange desire, mysterious to me now in her deep privacy, her strength, though that was not how I knew myself then.

"When she was mine"

Once, at Jack's invitation, not long after we'd met, I attended a play at his daughter's school. She was the star of the show, *Antigone*, her beauty and her talent on full display. I remember that when I came into the auditorium, a whole row of older women turned around and scowled at me, in unison, as fiercely as anyone ever has turned that glare in my direction. They were relations of Marie's—her mother, I think, and others. What had they been told that I was the object of such fury? Maybe I knew, or suspected, but I'd also been invited, with a friend (the tall slim one), to see the play, and we were invited to a party after the performance. Gina was sweet, welcoming. But the older women were all present and were sending daggers in my direction so I left the party shortly after arriving. I was learning what it was to have a whiff of scandal drifting in my wake.

In his conversations and his early letters, he stressed how his relationship with his daughter was one of mutual love and respect. He was innocent, he insisted, of any of the vile accusations made by parochial Victorians. (That whiff of scandal ...). I accepted this. Of course I did. I was twenty-three. In my experience, fathers did not engage in sexually charged relations with their daughters. In my experience. (In my experience, my father was not an object of desire. Nor was I to him. I would be surprised to learn he'd ever noticed my femininity apart from the one time he wondered what the bumps were under my T-shirt.) But later on in my life, I learned that incest was more common than I knew and that there were those who believed—who insisted they *knew*—that Jack was sexually involved with his daughter. Someone I met by chance much later, and who became a good friend for about eight years before he disappeared from my life, had been in a romantic relationship with Gina when they were both young actors. He said her father was a profound source of angst for her, in part because of what he had done when she was younger, and because her father wouldn't recognize the boundaries she needed to survive. In early letters, Jack wrote descriptions of his daughter's happiness with her first boyfriend:

> Gina, strolling home with her boyfriend's coat on. Eyes sparkling, very happy. Enjoyed her evening immensely. She tells me she likes him & *will* be seeing him again. I think she is going to have her first serious boyfriend. Life moves along. (May 5, 1978)

That boyfriend, who was Atom Egoyan, commented in an interview, years later:

> There was a young woman whom I adored from a very young age, and who was inaccessible to me for the longest time. Later on, it was revealed that there was an abusive relationship with her father. All the clues were there. But it wasn't a society at that point that could read them or respond to them, and I felt kind of helpless about it. So rather than address it, I went into denial, like everybody else. … I suppose the thing that confused it more than anything is that he himself was an artist, and it was so obvious what was going on, from the work he was doing and presenting publicly and the way he was behaving. But no one could actually talk about it. There was this incredible shroud of secrecy. And I was completely, madly in love with her. From about 13 to 18.[23]

To me, Jack celebrated his daughter's happiness with a boyfriend more or less her own age. But in the interview, the boyfriend described the landscape peopled with father, daughter and potential love interest quite differently, a young man in love and unable to talk to his beloved's father about a troubling issue:

> When the father realized I was serious about her, I had to make promises to him which I ultimately couldn't keep—in terms

> of keeping my relationship with his daughter platonic. It was a very strange time, because I was living a double life."[24]

Although she is not named, it is probable that the young woman Egoyan referred to was Gina.[25] She was alive when that interview appeared. So was Jack. In a piece written about her memorial event in Toronto, after her untimely death in 2010 from cancer at the young age of fifty, a writer describes Egoyan's moving testimony to Gina's influence on his work:

> Atom Egoyan sheepishly told about how as a boy his love for Gina prompted him to first immerse himself in the world of theatre, and to write plays, because he knew that was what Gina was interested in and he wanted to impress her. Ergo, it seems, Atom Egoyan's illustrious career was first sparked out of Gina Wilkinson's bright light.[26]

I came into the picture (that I posed for, took off my clothing for, felt uncomfortable within) at just the right time. It might have appeared that I replaced Gina as an obvious romantic partner, though I was certainly not that. There was a single kiss. In my mind, it was nothing I sought out, nothing I pursued, and I didn't feel it was a serious alliance with a future. Others felt differently, including Jack. Reading the letters now, I see the missed signals, the confessions, the plans.

The language Jack used about his daughter and their connection was strangely dated. Although he was proud of her and declared this repeatedly, he also lamented her independence when she went away to theatre school. And later, much later, he wrote of her relationship with a particular young man and referred to the time when "she was mine" (January 13–17, 1992).

Was I ever my father's? Would he have thought of me in that light? I suspect not.

In a very early letter to me, Jack said, "There is something I really want to say to you, it is in the back of my head, heart, somewhere. I don't want you to forget me. I want your feelings to grow, not shrink. I am selfish, I would try to make you dependent upon me" (May 1, 1978).

I pushed the question away

I didn't want to dwell on a story of sexual intimacy between a father and a daughter. I pushed the question away. Yet the topic came up, directly or by innuendo, in any conversation I had about Jack with others, in my meetings with him, his paintings of me. Innuendo was the light on a girl, almost a child, as she reached to push the door shut. In the drawings of long-haired beauties on a painter's lap, his brush twirling suggestively.

It was a story I was seeing elsewhere. In Michael Holroyd's biography of Augustus John, it's mentioned, almost in passing, that John slept with one of his daughters. Maybe two of them. And later, granddaughters. There were others. The English sculptor Eric Gill. The Austrian painter Egon Schiele, with a sister.

All these years later, as a mother and a grandmother, I am thinking again of the line between story and scandal, a line drawn with charcoal and smudged at times, faint, then dark. The line takes me to this moment, at my desk, with the book I've just finished reading, *Letters to Gwen John* by Celia Paul. Celia, for many years the lover of Lucian Freud (grandson of Sigmund). Gwen, her brother Augustus, Lucian, Celia, all painters I admire, maybe Gwen most of all.

> Gwen also suffered from memories of a darker intrusive intimacy, which made her afraid. In *Portrait Group* Augustus is standing beside a dark fireplace; the same fireplace appears in Gwen's portrait of their cleaning lady, Mrs. Atkinson, which reminds me of the dark fireplace in Lucian's portrait of Zoe Hicks. Zoe was Augustus's daughter. Lucian told me that Augustus had slept with Zoe, when he was an old man and she was a young woman. She also suggested to Lucian that Gwen's relationship with Augustus might briefly have been sexual, when they were both young.... As Michael Holroyd says in his biography of Augustus, when speaking of their cohabitation during the Slade years: "they dared not stay too close—there was the danger of emotional trespass with its trailing difficulties of guilt and regret."[27]

So many gazes, so many stories, so much pain, submerged or held to the body like a veil for shelter, meaning hidden in its folds. Let a body venture at last. But is it safe?

No one knew where I was

I wanted to disappear sometimes. When I was in my very early twenties, I spent a lot of my spare time alone. For four summers I worked at a busy tourist attraction. I almost always worked on weekends, in direct contact with hundreds of people, and had my two-day break midweek. I wanted quiet on those days and I often packed my green canvas rucksack and headed up the West Coast Road to a remote beach. I was convinced I was in love with someone I worked with, but he wasn't interested in me. The beach was as far away as I could get. I parked on the side of the road near Jordan River and hiked down a forest trail to a shore that felt like the edge of the world, and in some ways it was. On a clear day I could see to Cape Flattery on the Olympic Peninsula, the most northwestern point of the contiguous United States; beyond that, the lighthouse on Tatoosh Island, and then the wild Pacific all the way to Japan and beyond. On a clear night, the Tatoosh light, a smudgy yellow beam. My father had a small Primus Optimus stove I'd borrow for morning coffee and I'd make a beach fire for the comfort. I didn't bother much with food, apart from nuts and fruit, a few crackers. There was a spot above the high tide line where I could spread out my sleeping bag over sand and dry seaweed left by storms. All my sadness for the unrequited love and every other thing was recorded into a notebook, my longing kept at bay with brief dips in cold water. If I had a little run of days, more than two, I'd shower off the accumulated salt and woodsmoke under a sandstone ledge where the beach's namesake creek tumbled onto the sand. The first time I did this, I was astonished to see fossils in the sandstone—tiny fluted clamshells, ancient oysters, gastropods. I'd run my thumb along the rock and marvel at the archive of deep time I was standing near as I rinsed sweat and cedar smoke from my naked body. Mostly I didn't bother with clothes on these days unless others came to the beach, and there were never many people making the hike down a long trail from the highway. I kept a length of old curtain cloth I wrapped around myself. And I read books. Annie Dillard, Thomas Hardy, Greek plays in which everything was wild and poetic, the early collections of Seamus Heaney. Sometimes I wished for someone to share this with, but I felt calm in my own company. I'd tie shells to my ankles with long strands of seaweed, lick my shoulders for the salt. On the good days, I'd think how little it would take to make a life above the littoral zone. A shelter constructed of the logs and planks abundant on the beach. A fire. The luxury of a shower cavern dense with fossils. On the bad days, I was tempted to wade out into the chuck and let the tide take me. These two possible options were in balance. I'd come to the beach in despair or I'd come in joy. How little it would take, I thought, to make a life here.

One day at a very low tide, I walked around to the Jordan River estuary, rounding the point at the end of the beach and finding my way over rocks, through mud, eventually sitting on a log below the Breakers Cafe. Logging trucks raced by. I had a few dollars in my pocket and I walked over to the Jordan River Hotel—it was late morning by then—and went in to order a glass of cider. A couple of guys, regulars no doubt, wondered if I'd like to join them. They looked like they'd been drinking all night. I said no and sat at a table by a window overlooking the river. Beyond I could see that the tide had steadily crept in, surf washing over the rough grass of the foreshore. That meant walking back along the highway, up a switchback lined with leafy trees and blackberry canes reaching to the road. No one knew where I was. I thought about this, walking up the hot tarmac, skirting around fresh bear scats by the berry thickets.

On that length of shore, the wind coming off the Strait of Juan de Fuca, the smudgy light from Tatoosh, a few boats passing far out to sea, I was in an element where I was happiest, even when I was near to despair. Bedded down in sand above the high-tide line, naked in my sleeping bag, a bottle of Jameson settled into a ring of stones near the fire that smouldered quietly, surrounded by elegant driftwood as sculptural as anything by human hands, I was my own monument of selfhood, a true self. I felt I had been there before, not only a month or so earlier in the year, but in another life, an earlier life. Maybe I felt this as a protection against the world I was living in, an introvert who behaved badly in company. I wanted to belong to something other than that: a community, a place. In this place, among oystercatchers, sanderlings, cormorants, sandpipers, yellowlegs, herons fishing near the creek mouth, tracks of deer in the sand above my bed, eagles high, high, once a whale spouting not far from the shore, here, in this place, I was my own monument, a windblown grubby Kore. I needed no conscious reminder of who I was, no need to integrate the place and myself; the harmonies of water and land were my own consonance. I remember Freud's letter to Romain Rolland, discussing how the ego is defended by de-realization, and I want to find my way back to that beach, its bird cries, its solitude.

> It will be enough for my purposes if I return to two general characteristics of the phenomena of de-realisation. The first is that they all serve the purpose of defence; they aim at keeping something away from the ego, at disavowing it. Now, new elements, which may give occasion for defensive measures, approach the ego from two directions—from the real external world and from the internal world of thoughts and impulses that emerge in the ego.[28]

I have no images of myself at that remote beach, no paintings of myself standing under the cold water of the creek, my hands on the sandstone, moments when I felt more myself, an ongoing self. Naked, a broken whelk shell fastened to my sturdy ankle with a strand of fine seaweed. Was that my true self? Is the young woman holding a shawl over her head like a veil also my true self? I never thought about being seen on the beach. I sang. I never worried about being heard. Once I saw a bear walking around the rocks toward the estuary and realized he must have passed my little camp. I never thought about my body as an object. In that place I loved, it served me. I carried driftwood for my fire, rearranged logs for the perfect shelter, carried a kettle of water from the creek falling over the sandstone ledge back to my camp, swam strongly in the rough waves. Sometimes I danced. In no other place did I feel so at ease in the movement of my arms and legs, alone. "When is the burden of the gods lighter than air?"[29] wrote Camille Paglia, describing that porch of maidens, on the south side of the Erechtheion; inside, the ancient olive wood effigy of Pallas Athena, dropped from the heavens to earth. On a log by my sleeping bag, a twisted length of spruce root.

My father's age but not my father

But back to shame.

> Shame is the uncomfortable sensation we feel in the pit of our stomach when it seems we have no safe haven from the judging gaze of others.[30]

The painter wasn't the only one who gazed and judged. His gaze may have been more prurient than simply a formal evaluation of my body in a way that allowed him to recreate it on canvas, colour, texture and form. He may have been imagining the two of us on the flowered divan as he mixed his paints, outlined, worked on perspective. The flowered divan where I shivered but also, if I am honest, briefly enjoyed the focus of his gaze in those hours, or at least the first hours, before I realized how deep was his obsession. If I had given him any indication of my willingness, I think he would have put down his palette. I was not attracted to him but in the gaze I was beautiful, desirable. In retrospect, could I have found this in myself without his gaze lingering on me, stroking my body on the canvas with fine brushes, the touch of a finger? Could I have sourced my own beauty by turning inward?

> Anxious, guilty. The vaterkomplex of Freud at the Acropolis? The impossibility of existing without repeated legitimation (without books, map, family). Impossibility—depressing possibility—of "transgression."[31]

My father's age but not my father. Someone who looked at me naked and wasn't my father. Like Freud, I had ascended the Acropolis, in the company of young travelling mates, having never expected to see it, touch the pillars, breathe the same air as the Karyatids (for they were truly living, as alive as anyone gazing up at them), and did I suffer a "disturbance of memory"? I was not thinking of my father nor my mother, neither of whom had ever been in Athens, nor of my tangled and confused network of emotions related to them at that point in my life, a year and a half before I met Jack. In so much of my young womanhood, I felt I was transgressing the standards I'd been raised to respect, but I also felt that my own life would not be the life my parents had anticipated for me. In my role as a painter's model, perhaps I was remembering the five maidens of Karyai and their missing sister, alone in the British Museum after her removal by Lord Elgin in the first decade of the nineteenth century, their necks and shoulders strong enough to support the entablature of the Erechtheion. But their strength was foundational, structural; they might have been the subject of their creator's gaze, they are the object of our gaze, but their own eyes look out beyond us, whatever century we belong to.

The painter wasn't the only one to take my measure, to assess. I was also judged by my friends, young women, who urged me to lose weight, to behave in a more seemly way. By my mother, who felt I should wear more colour, cut my hair, gather in my loose ends of personality and intentions and find a path to the future that would include a nice boy, a ring on my left hand, wedding bells, a baby or two. I eventually had three, though I never wear a ring, not on any finger. And I learned I was most comfortably an introvert. Social occasions made, still make, me nervous and sometimes I drink too much to relax. I get loud, nervously garrulous, and tell the secrets of my heart to strangers. On the island off the Connemara coast, sometimes I'd go for weeks without seeing people because it was a small community, tightly knit, and I was considered a blow-in. They'd been driven to the island during the time of Cromwell and they'd learned to turn their backs to the world. When a young fisherman began visiting me, the one I wrote to two friends and my editor about, thus occasioning the news that I'd "netted" him, I thought that meant I might actually belong, but nothing was further from the truth. He wouldn't take me to kitchen parties but would stop by my dark cottage after midnight, emboldened by a few glasses of poteen.

Months later I met someone else, not from the island, who introduced me to his friends, but in the meantime, I lived without much contact with others and I learned that I enjoyed my own quiet company.

"I wish you near all the time"

In 1981, he found me again. It had been three years.

After I'd returned from Ireland, I'd begun to work part time in a bookstore so that I could spend half my time writing. Then, in February 1979, I met a poet, John Pass, at an event at Open Space in Victoria and we fell in love, marrying later that year. In 1981, we had the first of our three children. John taught at a community college and I was a graduate student at UBC. Our lives were rich and full.

A letter arrived from Jack: "For a long while I have wanted to tell you that I am happy to hear from Robin & Sylvia that your life continues to grow, that your art is blooming, & that you now have a child" (September 14, 1981). They must have given him my address, the one I shared with my new husband and baby son in North Vancouver. On the weekends we were building our house on the Sechelt Peninsula, the house we moved to a year later. He made contact. I must have responded because in a later letter, he mentions a card from me telling him that I'd gone to a show of his on Granville Street (I have no memory of this show) and he says he will be in Vancouver on particular dates for Royal Canadian Academy events and could we meet. Could he take me for lunch.

Stand back, well back, stand back and turn away, so that you are not looking at the paintings at all but remembering as clearly as you can the way you felt about the meetings, the letters. You were flattered, of course. You considered him, still consider him, to be a very fine painter. Some days you stop and look, seeing brushstrokes and composition, colour, and you know he was not a Sunday artist. It was everything to him. And in so many ways he was a good man. Generous, intelligent, interesting and all of these even more admirable traits when he was sober. When he drank he was unrestrained and excessive—the generosity too much, the intelligence overbearing.

It was a French bistro on Thurlow Street. I remember its interior—wainscotting, marble tables, wine in carafes. John and I had eaten there several times and I knew it was central. I brought my baby, who would have been seven months old. I probably had the fish soup. Jack sketched as we ate, drank wine (and yes, I felt some guilt, because of my child, but my glass kept being filled), and at one point, I had to feed my baby. It was an awkward moment because Jack was sitting so close and I was wearing a shirt I had to pull up rather than aside. I remember he ordered me chocolate mousse, which I ate quickly and happily, and before I knew it, there was another bowl of mousse in front of me. It wasn't exactly a gaze he directed at me, politicized and theoretical, but fierce scrutiny, taking in every part of me. He mostly ignored his meal but watched. He noted a small blemish by my eye. Shadows under them. I knew about these, of course. I had a baby, I was a graduate student at UBC, I was building a house on the weekends with my husband, I was writing whenever I could find a little opening of time. When I found a little opening of time, I liked to sit in the rocker my husband gave me for my birthday a few months before our baby was born, holding the baby asleep or nursing at my breast, thinking about poetry. The lists, the hectic drives across town to UBC, running stop signs and even lights sometimes so I wouldn't be late for class, the hectic rides back so I wouldn't be late for the babysitter, the urgent decisions about house details, dinners: I put those out of my mind as I sat, rocking my baby, sometimes making notes that became lines that became stanzas. His shoulders inspired a poem. His fingers. His blue eyes.

But now there was something more to add to the pressures of those days: the letters, which began to arrive too frequently, the phone calls, the requests for visits, for more of my time. Why couldn't I just drop everything and come to him? He needed to draw me, needed ... well, what he needed. Just after the day of the lunch visit, there was another day, maybe the following one, in which he also came to our house, had a drink, or probably several, and brought my husband a folio of drawings of naked women. He wrote, drunk ("a bit tight, squiffy, plastered, drunk," he confessed [November 7, 1981]), from the bus depot in Vancouver, eight pages of torrid prose ("I just love you and want to be with you forever—just the way it was in 1978"; "Dearest Theresa—what words I've written to you, what feelings you have generated in me! The terrible truth is that it is *all* true! You are my love, my counterpart. I am ... yours! You know this & fear it. You are right, my love, you are right" [November 7, 1981]), telling me he would watch over me, protect me, he would ask my husband to allow him to be by me at Halloween, at Christmas, at Easter, at Hay-time, at birthdays, christenings, marriages and funerals. And was my husband puzzled at this? I think he was. He was sympathetic and kind to the man who wrote these letters. I know there were other visits, later, in his Victoria apartment, John and I, with the baby or without (because my parents lived in the same city as he did and would babysit), and in our house, first in North Vancouver, and later on the Sechelt peninsula, for dinner or overnight. There was something resembling friendship and in the company of my husband, he was courtly, funny, and I felt lucky to know him. But if John left the room or I met Jack on my own or even within the pages of the frequent letters, there were undercurrents, undertow. What happened on the surface had an opposing force just beneath.

A folder arrived and within it, twenty pages: "My Life for Theresa Kishkan," begun on November 11, 1981, completed five days later. We'd had lunch on November 6, I see from its pages, so he'd returned home to Victoria and written an account of his life, detailing his early years, his time at art school and, in a section about his loves, every significant relationship or attraction from the age of nine to the present. ("The condemned man striving to cram as much information onto paper before the dawn."[32])

He described several of the attractions as recognitions of his archetype. His wife, his daughter ("She was very much my archetype & not only physically, but intellectually, she enchanted me") and me. ("In March 1978 met & instantly fell in love with a young poet. She was twenty-three, very beautifully my archetype.... I became in a blink enchanted! After three months, during which time she dominated every moment of my life, she left for a stay in Ireland.")

His letters, which were fulsome in their praise, also had a pressure current running through them. "Habit is an insidious thing. I noticed that this Friday. I went to my mailbox anticipating a letter from T, and the twinge of disappointment that followed" (February 28, 1982). Once he admits to thinking I am probably tired. (Even a muse gets tired.) I felt responsible to some extent for his happiness, and although this was my problem to deal with, to get beyond, I was vulnerable to pressure because I was tired and too busy and trying hard to do my best, more than my best, to do well with the challenges I was facing: university work, house-building, motherhood, my relationship with my husband, the frequent phone calls from my mother and my mother-in-law, warning me not to take on so much. Some days I was so tired that I wanted to daydream about sleep, knowing that sleep itself was impossible during the long and broken hours.

In a letter written on May 11, 1982, he wrote that he was giving me the *Mother and Child* painting. At our lunch at the French bistro, he'd been sketching. I can't find a reference in the letters of him working on this particular canvas, but the painting he'd intended to give me, one he'd referred to earlier as *The Dreamer*, wasn't as significant as the *Mother and Child*. Or that was his rationale for giving me the *Mother and Child*.

The cruciform wainscotting, just behind the table where we ate our lunch, my dark hair, my left shoulder trying to shield me—us, because look how my hand cradles my baby's head—my right arm abstracted and awkward (I *was* awkward, trying to feed my baby while knowing that every inch of me, every move I made, every gesture, was observed and recorded), my eyes meeting my baby's eyes, not the observer's. He didn't miss a thing. He wrote the torrid letter after ("I wish you near all the time"), but whatever he felt was gracefully set aside to allow this painting. It's me but it's also more than me. *Virgo Lactans*, the nursing Madonna. The tradition of the nursing Madonnas arose in a way to humanize the Virgin, to show her as a mother with a child, to portray her as a mother like any mother, feeding her child from her body.

> Head reclining, nape finally relaxed, skin, blood, nerves warmed up, luminous flow: stream of hair made of ebony, of nectar, smooth darkness through her fingers, gleaming honey under the wings of bees, sparkling strands burning bright ... silk, mercury, ductile copper: frozen light warmed under fingers.[33]

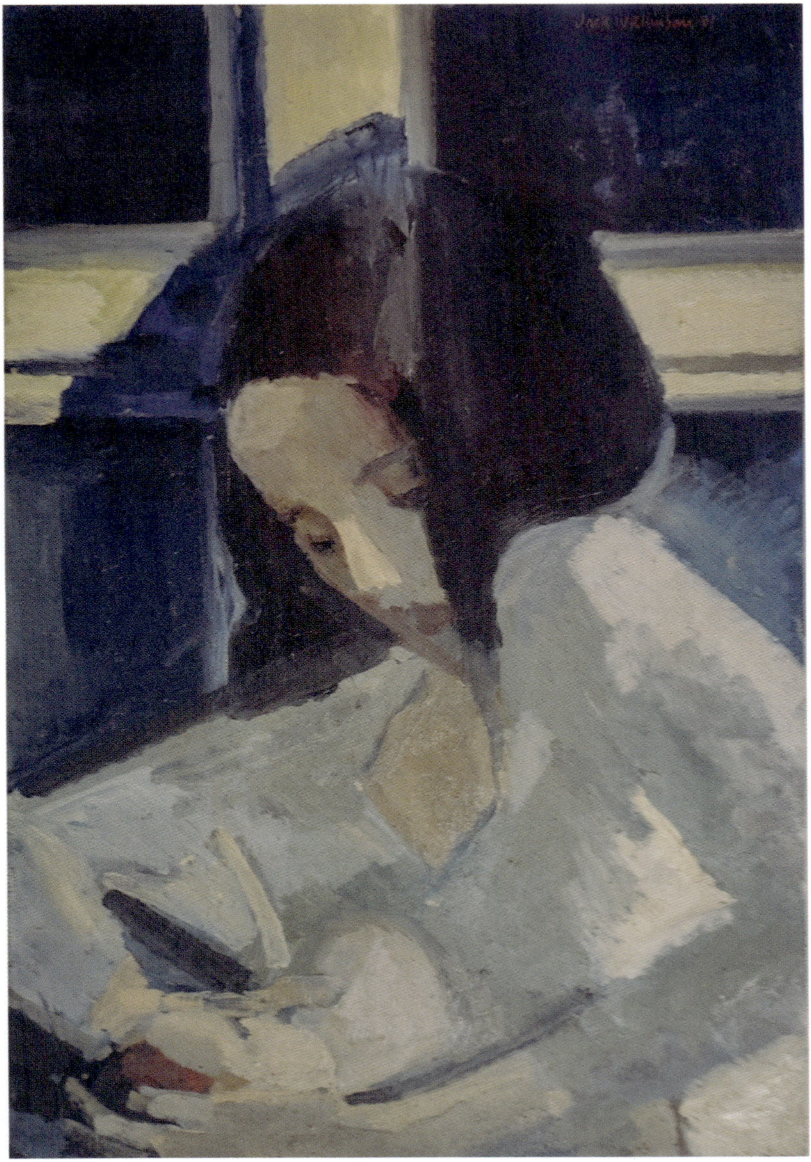

The painting attempts to place me in a devotional context rather than an erotic one. Or does it? I wonder. All these years I've looked at it as restrained and perhaps elegant, a profound moment of love between a mother and her child. But reading the letters that followed the meeting that inspired it—now I'm not so sure. The creamy breast, the fall of dark hair, these painted, and painted again, using this palette, in the image of me with a shawl or kimono over my shoulders, the artist in his black hat and clipped beard putting a brush to canvas, two brushes in his left hand poised against the model's (*my*) thigh.

His gaze

Sometimes I felt his gaze on me as I rode my bike to work, sat at my desk thinking my way into poems, and later, much later, drank coffee by our woodstove in a beautiful silk robe given to me by a wonderful woman, a robe he never saw. I felt his gaze pinning me to paper like a bright butterfly. For years afterwards, a gaze followed me, whatever I did. "A coy black-haired girl wearing a vermilion red gown, on a green mauve ground with a pale summer green light from a window" (May 22, 1982). I was never her, never had a vermilion gown in pale summer light, and I never knew I could refuse the gaze. Until he was dead and I was too old.

> The time for comprehending can be reduced to the instant of the glance, but this glance can include in its instant all the time needed for comprehending.[34]

"I don't want you to forget me"

> The second general characteristic of the de-realisations—their dependence upon the past, upon the ego's store of memories and upon earlier distressing experiences which have since perhaps fallen victim to repression—is not accepted without dispute.[35]

The past is both a store of memories and a repression. I think of Freud's visit to the Acropolis and how it resulted in him musing on his distant relationship with his father. A forgetting. A disputation of facts. Reading the stack of letters I'd put away in a drawer, I realize I'd forgotten how excessive was Jack's expression of love. His detailed accounts of the women in his life while insisting on my importance. The off-putting descriptions of his infatuation with young girls. With his daughter. I was complicit in this. I must have been. I say now that what I felt for him was friendship and—at first—admiration. What I felt from him was love, care and also obsession, though I wasn't exactly a young girl. In a letter just before I left for Ireland, he'd written that he wanted me to be dependent. He needed to be the focus, the centre of my orbit.

And while I was on the flight there, a letter was also travelling to greet me on my arrival:

> One hell of a black day, all of it loneliness, sadness, and loss, swept into a pile of regret in my system...The truth is, Theresa, I'm almost unbearably sad. I'm trying to do everything I can to rid myself of this heavy feeling. I feel a little mad. (Insane.) (May 5, 1978)

I'd forgotten how there was a dark shadow in my life for days after the letters arrived. "I don't want you to forget me." He made forgetting impossible. A sustained pressure, difficult to repress. Even from thousands of miles away, on an island without electricity or running water, where I sat on rocks looking out on the wild Atlantic, wondering what it would be like to slip into the ocean unseen. (I would never have to pick up another letter from the post office, my name in his bold dark script.) I felt I could not possibly do the right thing, whatever I did. Write back, or let the pages flutter away in the wind. He made forgetting impossible and I was learning how shame could occupy such space in a body and mind.

I felt shame when I looked inward. What had I done, who was I, that someone noticed me across a room and had his life turned upside down as a result. Was it something I wore, something I said, or was it me, pure and simple? Or not so pure and simple, but something integral to my person? When the letters arrived, I felt the tiny community where I lived in a small cottage on my own, quietly, and I thought purposefully, must know that I was not a good person but someone who could cause such anguish to someone else. The envelopes themselves, addressed in a distinctive black script, vibrated with his intensity, his focus on me. I was guilty, yes I was, I must be, I was certain of it: for who I was, what I had set in motion when I arrived at an opening for an exhibition in my peacock skirt. And for agreeing to take off my clothes for an older artist whose intentions were perhaps not entirely honourable.

A stack of letters arrived in the mail. An elegant notebook with "Five Letters to Theresa" inscribed on a title page and then the letters themselves, beginning somewhat formally and then spiralling into obsessive stuff, a little book he prepared for me with artistic advice (I was taking some materials with me to Ireland but wasn't sure how to use them) and that similarly spiralled.

> I love Theresa K. I'm not scheming to get her to bed. I want her in so many more ways than that! Most of all, I want her trust, her friendship, her love. It wouldn't be very important even if she did go to bed with me. Sex reduces

> us all to "poodle dogs" as Pablo P was wont to observe. I'd like to see her body tho'.[36]

Partly, I didn't know how to say no. Partly, if I'm honest, I didn't want to. There was something to find out, I thought. About myself, about the experience, even about the future.

> If I have rightly guessed the meaning of the thought that came to me on the Acropolis and if it did in fact express my joyful astonishment at finding myself at that spot, the further question now arises why this meaning should have been subjected in the thought itself to such a distorted and distorting disguise.[37]

When I stop at the foot of the stairs to talk to my younger self, it's unsettling. Is she the shadow or am I? Some mornings there's a glare on the glass and I can't see her face clearly. Her eyes are deep and dark. And not evasive exactly, but remote. Her mouth is slightly pursed. Although she has small blossoms scattered in her hair, apple blossoms or jasmine, something white and virginal, she isn't happy about the time it is taking to make her image, though I know Jack worked from a photograph. She is not giving much. Don't ask me to smile, I imagine her thinking. Don't get too close.

"I love your courage," he wrote, "your tenacity. I know you have talent, though its dimension is temporarily obscured by the 'novelty' phase of your life. You are gathering experience. I feel for you. Can you understand that, accept me?"[38] What he called courage—in a letter in November 1978—I would have called a challenging fear, not courage. I never felt I had inner strength. I went to Ireland on my own, and before that to Europe alone (because the couple I arrived in Spain with soon moved on), because I wanted to find out how to do these things alone. No one else I knew wanted to join me and I thought if I waited, life would get in the way. I would never know what it was to travel to an unknown place with only my own resources to depend on, in those days before cell phones, computers, text messages. It wasn't courage. I was often scared of what might happen, of what might not. In train stations, holding a ticket, I'd count and recount my traveller's cheques, work out yet again the train time, given using the twenty-four-hour clock, to make sure I knew when to board, when I'd arrive in Menton or Brindisi or Barcelona.

And what did he mean, "temporarily obscured by the 'novelty' phase of [my] life"? I suspect he was waiting. Waiting for me to discover it was him I really wanted, his absorbing interest and involvement, and not my independence—a small flat on Fort Street, a part-time job working in a bookstore, riding my bike in all weather, planning a return to Ireland once I could save enough money, walking late at night down dark streets to the sea. Through him my "talent" would flourish, realize its true and full dimension. In his care, his keeping, draped in a Japanese veil or with flowers scattered in my hair. I was twenty-three. I'd written two collections of poetry, had almost completed a novella and was writing more poems. What was the novelty? I was quite sure this would be my life, as it was, and is now. Writing, a life.

"I felt his scrutiny intensify"

Reading Celia Paul's *Self-Portrait*, more than forty-five years after I'd taken off my clothes and tried to relax on a flowered counterpane, I am taken back, back, through time:

> Lucian placed the easel near the bed. He stood very close to me and peered down at me. I was very conscious of my flesh, and I felt myself to be undesirable.... When he first started the painting I was lying on the usual off-white counterpane. The first marks he made were depictions of my nose and mouth. He worked outwards gradually. He admired the "rhubarb" pink of my fingers next to my face. When he came to painting my breasts, I felt his scrutiny intensify.[39]

The painting that resulted, *Naked Girl With Egg*, reminds me a little of a painting of me I can't find now, in any gallery or private collection, not because the paintings are similar—they aren't—but because of the way the breasts still hold the painters' gaze after so many years. In mine, I am tanned, almost like a young Tahitian woman out of a Gaugin canvas, the wild flowers of the counterpane a bright contrast to my skin, and my breasts are enormous. (Were they that large then, before children, before aging filled out my body to something resembling my grandmother's?) In Celia's, she is holding one breast from beneath, uplifting its weight; the other breast, her right, falls to one side. The counterpane she mentions has become black, not off-white. Two poached eggs in a little ramekin sit on a low table, a small meal waiting for her modelling session to conclude. Marie brought me tea and a biscuit during mine.

"I am trying to cover tracks that could lead to you"

It was perhaps 1983 or '84 when I decided to make a linocut for John to print as a Christmas card. We had—*have*—a nineteenth-century Chandler and Price platen press. We hadn't yet printed anything but type, but if the linocut I was attempting turned out, we thought it would be something to try on the press. I remember sitting at the kitchen table with the box of tools we'd bought, a piece of lino and an idea. I wanted to try to make our house on its hill as a nod to the name we used for the work we'd done on our press, poetry broadsheets for a literary market: High Ground. We thought it also worked as a name for our home. We liked its sense of optimism. Our house on its bluffs facing west, built with love and hope. Our young family. Our writing lives. I sat with the tools, the image I had in mind sketched on the lino with a tentative pencil, a few smudgy areas where I'd rubbed out a line. Now what?

Jack called. Sometimes his phone calls were difficult, particularly the ones he made when he'd had a few too many glasses of Jameson whiskey. It was hard to keep the conversation light. But this time it was morning and he'd simply called from Victoria to say hello. I told him what I was doing, was trying to do, and he was delighted. Making art! I explained I wasn't really making art because I didn't know how to begin the cutting. He was very helpful. He told me to warm the lino to make it more pliable and easier to cut. He told me which tools to use for what part of the work and he said how much he looked forward to the card. I cut and scraped away the surface and John printed the resulting block. There was a bit of cross-hatching I knew immediately was a mistake, an error in design, but otherwise I was thrilled with the cards. I remember sending one to Jack and having him send, in return, a small linocut print, in two colours, rust red and blue.

Reading the letters again, at my desk during a cold winter week leading up to Christmas, taking a break from making this year's linocut, I find a narrative I hadn't realized was there. From the first letter to the last. The earliest thread is how he fell in love with me at first sight. At first glance, first gaze, and how that affected him in the first weeks.

> The past eight weeks have been, have contained, some of the tenderest, bitter-sweet moments

> of my life. Also, some of the most frustrating. I don't think I have ever thought of anyone, in detail, so much, ever, in my long life. You have, quite literally, filled my thoughts since Mar. 3rd. Quite an experience for a man of fifty. I've thought a lot about that too—too much, maybe. I don't care really, that you are twenty-three, thirty-three, thirteen, etc. (May 1, 1978)

Five Letters to Theresa began as a series of texts about his belief in me as an artist, in his own philosophy of art and love, and then it quickly became an imploring, highly emotional plea for me to remain, to love him. And then the words ran out, turned into drawings of me, my face, my body (clothed and unclothed), dreamy portraits and embarrassing vignettes of lovers separated by wind, chasms and so on. I remember beginning to read the letters and then closing the book quickly because was this really me he was talking to? Even then, the life he was dreaming of, proposing we embark upon together, felt so unexpectedly serious and utterly not one I was interested in living. ("Theresa, know this. I love you and I'll never cause you, knowingly, any harm. Theresa, can't we be as dear to one another as life will permit? If circumstance will not allow you to be my true lover, be my dearest friend, forever."[40]) Now that I am a grandmother, no longer the girl with the dark hair and opulent breasts he drew obsessively, I read the letters again and understand how he tried to coax me into making a life with him. "I would try to make you dependent upon me" (May 1, 1978).

The epistolary narrative provides me with a story I tried not to take to heart, *my* heart, though now it has entered like a delayed arrow. An arrow caught in the years but finally finding its mark.

"A form of exorcism"

The gaze that observed her, detailed her body, her ballet training, her sprawl on her bed with a floppy hat, a pubis without hair, then with it. The gaze that lingered on her breasts, her lovely face, her skin creamy with morning light. A gaze that never left her, never left her alone. A line beginning, charcoal or ink, the paper fine Ingres, a line beginning, pausing as the artist in his hat pauses, mid-stroke, continuing, her body on the surface on the paper, high cheekbones, long eyes, her dark hair; a line continuing, shading here, a cheek turned away, rubbed, returned, continuing until she is there, not exorcised at all, but shapely in the ink, the charcoal (though she is no longer alive).

In the essay Jack wrote for me to provide me with what he considered the pivotal moments of his life, he described falling in love with his daughter. He described his sexual attraction to her. "The blunt expression of sensuality," he said, "was read as incest" by the public who viewed his paintings of Gina. "When she was mine," he wrote, in retrospect, lamenting her move to her own life. The artist and model theme he regarded "as a form of exorcism," but what father exorcises attraction by painting his daughter over and over, the gaze of ownership, this time with himself in a Renaissance hat, his paintbrush, feathers brandished as a promise, a threat, a sex toy?

And after her, it was me. A different hat, or maybe the same one, the brush extended.

His wife, Marie, was nice to me

His wife, Marie, was nice to me, when I visited Jack's studio, when I stopped by for lunch on one occasion, at his invitation. She was elegant, gracious, and welcomed me into her home, or at least that's how I remember it. Yet I think I must have hurt her, without consciously knowing that I could. Now, reading the letters again, discovering the narrative I'd somehow missed, I feel shame and guilt in the realization of how I was implicated in the end of Jack's marriage. Embedded. In no small way culpable. "Shame makes us direct our focus inward and view our entire self in a negative light."[41] Was I willing to be implicated in what became a mess? I know now that I wasn't able to take a distanced view of the drama playing out by letter, phone call, quiet tables in small bars overlooking the sea. When he told me that our friendship was in no way a threat to his marriage or that, once the marriage came apart, that I was in no way responsible, I initially accepted these assurances at face value. It wasn't a situation I sought out, I didn't pursue him, apart from opening the first letter, agreeing to meet him. "Guilt causes us to focus our attention on the feelings of others."[42] From the other side of this long stretch of years, decades, nearly half a century, I look into my heart and its nest of memories and I am ashamed that I took so little care of his wife's feelings. Later I learned she was compromised by her own hidden infidelity and might have been relieved to have Jack's attentions directed elsewhere. I hadn't had any experience with a situation such as this one, but still, I was callous, unthinking. I should never have opened that first envelope, never responded, never visited his home, allowed him to paint me, draw me, take me for meals, flatter me, cajole me into a friendship that he obviously hoped would be more. I should never, never, never.

He wrote from a dark place: "I am, for the first time in my life, using prescribed medication for almost chronic & rather severe depressions. For the first time I seem to be out of control of myself & do not understand what is happening ... You are in no way, responsible for my misery & I will be hurt if you in any degree assume such a thing" (June 14, 1978). But he wrote long letters describing his loneliness, the breakup of his marriage, the ambivalence of his sons, and I let this weigh upon my conscience because of course I was responsible. Wasn't I? Alone on an Irish island, there was no one I could talk to about this.

In a letter written to me in Ireland, regarding a drawing he'd made of me to give to my parents:

> I did not give Meg one for your parents because I am trying to cover tracks that could lead to you. Marie was very hurt by my attraction to you & I don't intend this to be used as a reason for our separation. (June 18, 1978)

And later, after their separation:

> Marie came out to the airport with me, was looking thro' my hurriedly collected things thrown into my bag—came across your book—became upset. Yet I love her in a way that is so different to my feelings for you. You or she can't understand that! (January 9, 1979)

What was I to understand? I wanted no part of their difficult relationship, no part in it. I was making my own way in life at that point, having returned from Ireland, looking for work, trying to find a way to write in a serious and committed way, and I had no interest in renewing a regular friendship with Jack. Let my tracks stay covered, I thought. Or did I? Did I even recognize that was the undercurrent? In another letter, anticipating my return from Ireland, he urged me to come see him, saying, "I know that it is a little difficult for you—for me, I only want to sit and talk, get near to you" (November 17, 1978). This is a letter I'd completely forgotten, perhaps out of self-defence. I didn't believe for a minute that he would agree to a mild friendship. In an earlier letter, he had said,

> Perhaps you were the first friend I'd encountered in a long while & I *made* it into something else, because you are beautiful. I'd like to be your friend & when & if you return, I hope that we will be able to see each other, on that basis. I'll never embarrass, or frighten, you again. (I did, didn't I?) (July 26, 1978)

I never told him where I lived.

And now? I have to wonder why he told me about his (ex-)wife's feelings if he wasn't somehow hoping that I might feel enough guilt to see him again?

His feelings, her feelings: I was too careless. And now I am left with my feelings, which are complicated, all-consuming on this December day when I am at my desk, reading old letters, looking at drawings of myself and realizing how little I'd thought about consequences. I didn't know I had to.

> If you *were* free of all assignments, projects, part time jobs, etc., & I, too, could do as I please, I would spend all my time with you. When you are here, I hate the way the time seems to fly, the way that visitors, etc., interrupt my concentration upon you.[43]

In my defence, if I need one (though perhaps for a time, unknown to me, I might have needed one; a case was being prepared to suggest I had alienated the affection of a husband for a wife), my feelings were never what his were. I did not want to be dependent on him, did not want to share my life with him, fill his days with my presence. I did not want his "concentration." I did not love him. Yet in his letters, professions of love fill the pages, love that his wife understandably believed rightly was part of their marital bond. She might have hoped to have me legally declared a home-wrecker. That was what he was suggesting to me. Yet when I look at the BC Family Law Act now, I realize that his fears about tracks leading to me, fears he wanted me to take on, couldn't have amounted to anything. (Oh, the drama of an aging painter in love with a young poet.)

> While a handful of states still allow the tort of alienation of affections, it is not a tort in Canada. In British Columbia's *Family Law Act*, the provincial legislation that governs spouses and the breakdown of relationship, this cause of action is barred by s.196.[44]

How blithely I went about my own days, or it seemed so, though in truth I was not always blithe because nothing in my life had prepared me to be the object of such obsessive love. But I never hesitated for a moment to proceed with the plans I'd already made. A flight, the search for a cottage I wrote about earlier, and time, time to find myself as a writer, to learn to enjoy my own company, for despite a few romantic entanglements, I was mostly alone. I did pack the little painting set Jack gave me, and his notes on colour, perspective and other considerations. I bought some canvas paper in Galway, along with a few tubes of colour I knew I wanted to use to try to paint the otherworldly place where I was living, with its soft grey Irish mist, soft green fields, dark bricks of turf cut from the bogs, and weather-beaten whitewashed cottage surrounded by grey-green leaves. The ocean just below my step, glittering. What remains is a single painting I gave to my parents as a gift when I returned home and that I have in my home now, after their deaths.

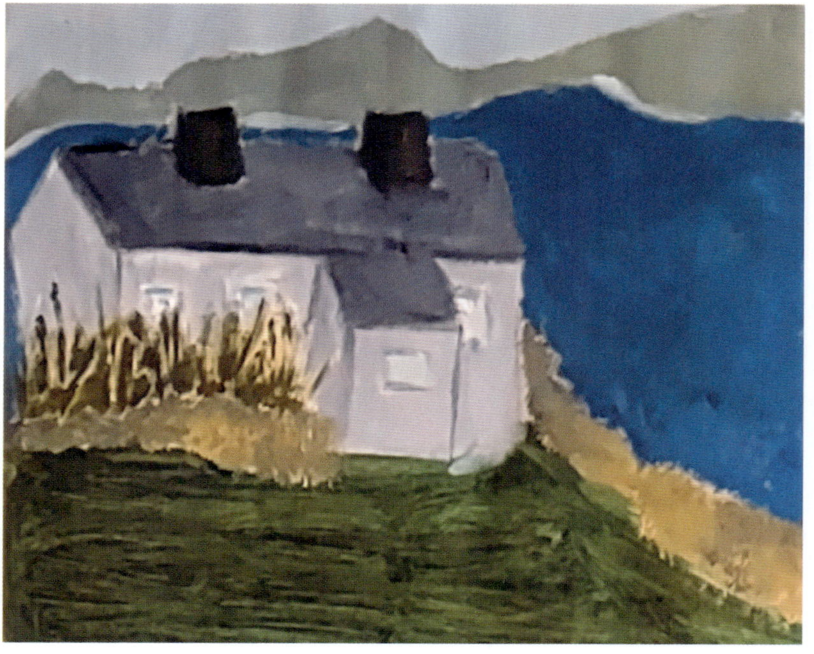

I remember how I was filled with the need to put the image down, without any real skill or knowledge. I sketched the cottage with its hedge of elephant grass, its green field, the beach below, the deep blue of the water between the island and Eyrephort strand in the distance, and then tried to mix paints accordingly. Every element of the painting is clumsy and awkward yet somehow it carries something of how I felt about the cottage that was my home for many months. Months in which I experienced dread whenever a letter arrived with the bold dark handwriting. He couldn't ever find me here, could he? I was free of him. Or was I? I tried to put him out of mind. I didn't miss his attention. It had become a source of anxiety, dread. His voice on the phone, coaxing me to come out to meet him for a meal, a walk, to sit in his cold studio without my clothes while he peered and dabbed paint on a stretched canvas. In the last days, and when I thought of those days thousands of miles away on an island in the wild Atlantic, I was stretched beyond my emotional limits until I found my own quiet self again.

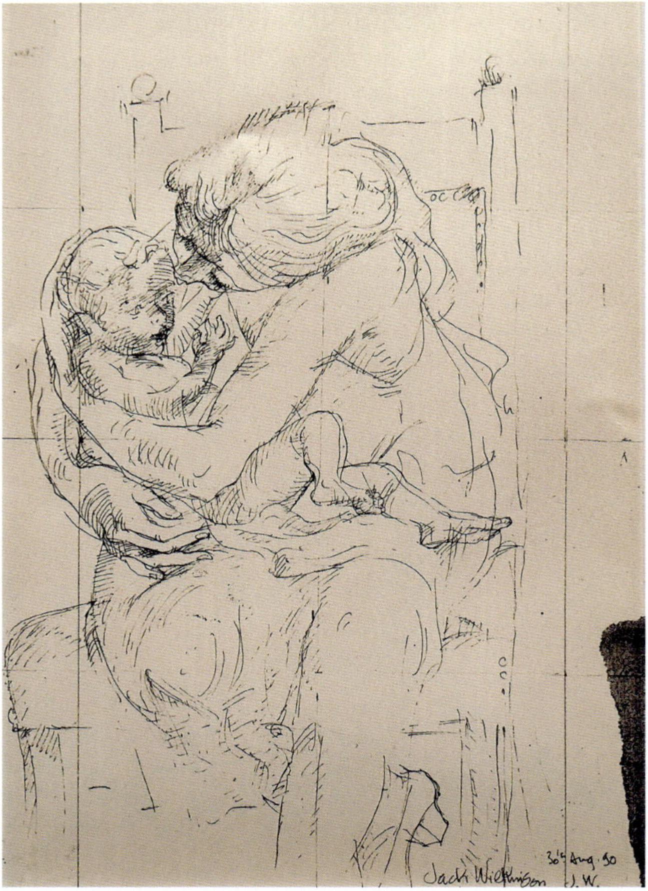
30th Aug. 90
Jacki Wilkinson
J.W.

"On hair falling down in curls"

Section 389 of Leonardo da Vinci's notebook:

> On hair falling down in curls:
> Observe the motion of the surface of the water which resembles that of hair, and has two motions, of which one goes on with the flow of the surface, the other forms the lines of the eddies; thus the water forms eddying whirlpools one part of which are due to the impetus of the principal current and the other to the incidental motion and return flow.[45]

He drew me once with my third child. He drew on rough paper that began to deteriorate almost at once. He made a copy and brought it when he came for a visit. It's on the wall outside my study and I see it every time I come in to work at my desk. When he brought it, I almost forgot the difficult weeks, the letters, the pressure, the insistent pronouncements of love. Look at my strong arms, the drapery of my clothes, the soft curl of my hair down my back, like water in motion. Look at my hands.

I almost forgot.

"And how can body, laid in that white rush, But feel the strange heart beating where it lies?"[46]

In my cottage on the edge of the Atlantic, the smell of iodine entering my dreams at night, corn crakes creaking in the long grass, I read poetry. I read Yeats, whose work I'd studied at university and who was part of the reason I'd come to the west of Ireland, his lines tangled up with old reels and Synge's journals, and as I was reading, a poem spoke directly to me.

> Did she put on his knowledge with his power
> Before the indifferent beak could let her drop?[47]

What was it about Jack's letters, his insistence on seeing me, his *insistence*?

> Now, in this tiny space in my life, when with intuitive comprehension, I recognize you, all I want, all I need, really, truly, is to be near you, to see you.[48]

I liked his paintings. I liked talking to him. His attention made me uncomfortable. He was never indifferent. But his heart was strange.

"under a veil of words"[49]

There were so many words. There still are. A stack of letters on my desk, many of them fifteen or twenty-five pages, written on fine Arches paper or torn from a diary or on hotel stationery; a notebook of painting advice quickly changing to declarations of eternal love; twenty pages of his life given to me in a brown paper folder; a volume of formal letters now in a university collection (letters scanned for me by a kind librarian because I'd already included the volume with my other papers, not foreseeing I might need to read them again); my own letters somewhere, or nowhere, of no use to the dead and forgotten by the living. Burn them, the therapist tells me, when I confess I will send the stack of letters and the notebook to the university to join my papers there once I am finished this book. You don't have to share them with anyone, she insists. But I am venturing out of the shelter I have kept to with my feelings and complicated shame, hidden in the hermitage of something like remorse or regret, and the letters are all the words I didn't read carefully enough but have attended to now, in this conversation with myself. My selves. The older one, and I hope wiser, though still not at home in a large body, its awkward strength. The younger self, whom I didn't love enough, judged unfairly in her gauzy veil, her ample flesh, her hair starred with jasmine, her averted gaze.

"a coy black-haired girl wearing a vermilion red gown, on a green mauve ground with a pale summer green light from a window"

Jack gave my son Brendan a painting to celebrate his birth. On the back, he wrote an inscription, wishing Brendan a happy life. He wrote that the image was his mother. And I recognize my face and head, though in so many ways it isn't me. In a letter on June 11, 1982, written seven months before Brendan's birth, describing the painting that he would gift to my child, he wrote,

> The girl from the magazine photo in the vermilion red gown, with the summer green

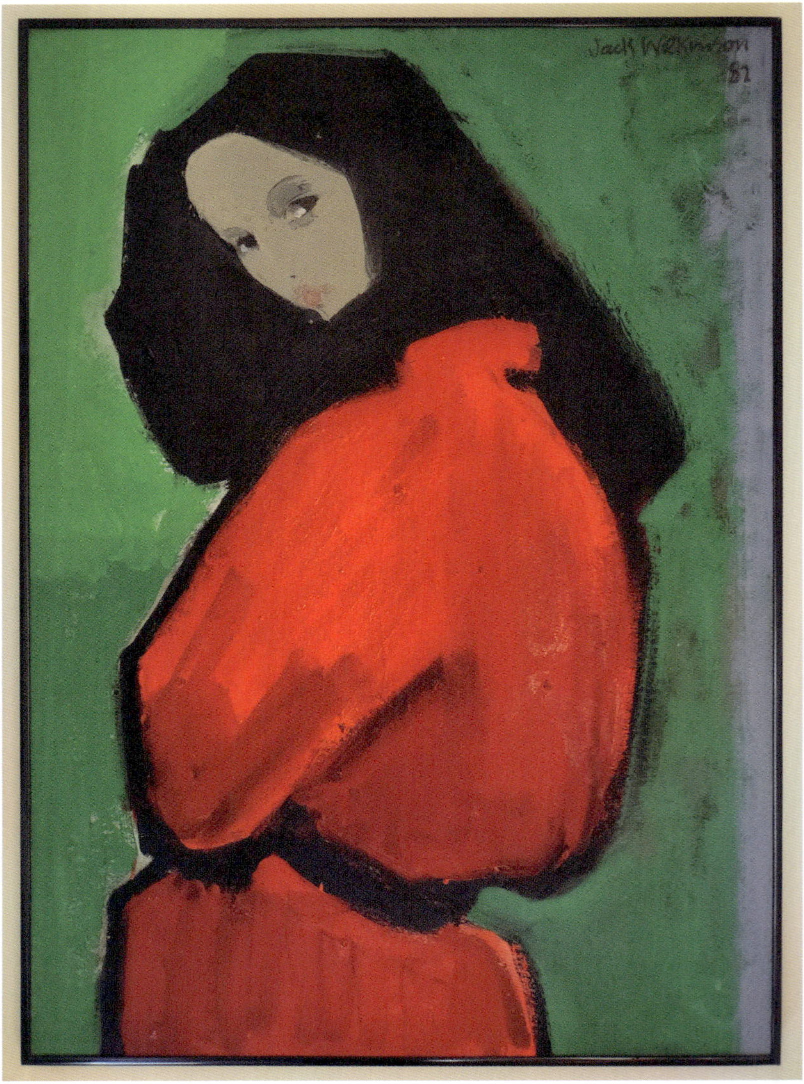

> window, becomes you, sultry, looking over your shoulder. The vermilion becomes magenta, the ground becomes plum & the perfectly easy head (from the photo) becomes difficult and special as I struggle with a personal image. I've painted it a dozen times.

Somewhere in the letters, I remember him showing this painting at a private sale in his home and reporting that Sylvia Skelton said, "Oh, yes, that's Theresa." But was it? Is it? Maybe the one that he gifted to Brendan isn't the one she saw. ("I've painted it a dozen times.")

I can't say I ever knowingly cast that come-hither look over my shoulder. (But remember, I'd disappointed him by not accepting his advances, so no doubt he'd imagined the look, a cock-tease, an unfulfilled promise.) Nor is my waist so neat and slim. But hers is the same face as the one that greets me at the foot of the stairs every morning, her high forehead, her dark eyes and hair. Hold the pose, shrug your shoulders, gaze out as though to say, I don't really mean this. This is not who I am. But at least I'm dressed. Looking at the painting now, I see another look on my face, warning the painter off, and I am reminded of Gina, closing her door.

Earlier he'd described the painting in a letter: "a coy black-haired girl wearing a vermilion red gown, on a green mauve ground with a pale summer green light from a window" (May 22, 1982). What someone intends and the result—there is a stretch of time, of imaginary time, in imaginative space.

> The views of space and time which I wish to lay before you have sprung from the soil of experimental physics, and therein lies their strength. They are radical. henceforth, space by itself, and time by itself, are doomed to fade away into mere shadows, and only a kind of union of the two will preserve an independent reality.[50]

Maybe I was the inspiration for this work, but I didn't travel across the space-time continuum, apart from my hair. And perhaps my eyes. Instead of mathematics, pigments and graphic structure were the elements.

Stand in your robe, waist cinched tight, and look to the present, when I am waiting for my son to claim his painting, supposedly his mother; it is stored behind a desk for the moment, those eyes open but temporarily without anything to see. It is a portrait of time, of what was and what was to come.

Let the body venture forth

> My love for her is intense but not perverse.
> I lived my life with her as my companion
> at least from 1970–77. Every moment with
> her was happiness to me. To hold her hand
> & walk a beach was the greatest joy to me.
> How right or wrong it was, I can't judge.[51]

She was beautiful, his daughter. She filled the room with her beauty, her vibrant voice, her passion for the stage, for conversation. On a walk one winter afternoon, around Christmas, with my husband and Jack and me, she suddenly dashed into a little corner store on Cook Street in Victoria and came out with her arms filled with flowers. On the grey street, her hair under a bright hat, the scent of freesias, the sound of her laughter.

By then she was living elsewhere, home for the holiday. In his apartment, one floor of an old house on Cook

Street, two beds were side by side in the bedroom, the width of my hand apart. How right or wrong it was, I can't judge. (But I do.)

What do you know about that time, I ask

> The very same impressions that we have forgotten have nonetheless left the deepest traces on our minds.[52]

One thing I realized after spending two weeks rereading the stack of letters dating from 1978 until 1997 was that certain assumptions I held about a group of men I'd known weren't exactly true. I thought I'd had friendships with them, that they cared for me in ways that didn't involve sexual interest or competition, and that among them, I was one of them. I was invited to their Friday evenings when they'd gather in the library of a publishing company and drink whiskey together. They'd tell stories, talk about books. I thought I was there because they liked me and not because they had intentions or hopes.

I am not putting this very well. Reading the letters, I was surprised and yes, *say it*, I was hurt to read that conversations among themselves about me, written down for me by Jack, indicated the level of their care was pretty low.

> I'd heard about your "fishy" adventures
> from Dick Morriss. I was seeing him about
> printing some drawings for me, your name
> entered into the conversation. D.M. said
> he'd heard from you, that you were enjoying your stay in Ireland & that you had been
> netted by a fisherman. (July 26, 1978)

A couple of things: Dick Morriss was my publisher. I don't remember the letter I wrote to him but I would imagine it had to do with a forthcoming book. (I'd been asked via someone else to make sure the publisher had an address to send me the page proofs for my book. This was before computers and the island I was living on didn't have electricity; there was only one telephone, in the living room of the house that served as a post office.) The term *fishy* implies suspicious or devious behaviour. It is also sexual in the worst way, implying the scent of bodies after prolonged lovemaking. Was this what they really thought of me? Jack because I had essentially terminated his attentions? The publisher for his own reasons? This little exchange also reminds me of something else, that Robin Skelton, the poet who'd edited my book (who was also a visual artist and a Limner) asked me if I'd consider using one of Jack's drawings, perhaps even one of the ones Jack was arranging to have printed by Dick Morriss, on the cover of my next book. (Jack brought my husband a folio of drawings as a gift the second time they met. In each drawing, the model was naked. She looked like me but it was only by reading the dates that I realized he'd given John the first folio he created, containing drawings of Gina; a second, comprising drawings of me, was the one Jack was referring to in his letter to me in Ireland.) I was uncomfortable at this suggestion, though I didn't think too deeply about my reasons then, and simply insisted we use something more appropriate to the themes of the poems in the book. I didn't think too deeply. Did I even intuit then that their gaze was not unlike Jack's? That in their gaze I was unclothed, sultry, maybe even available? To any of them, or maybe just one? I don't think I did intuit that, but I should have. It pains me to write this. For years I have kept these suspicions well suppressed. Bringing them out to the light of day makes me feel dirty, recognizing in the smile of benevolence the shadow of a leer. I am ashamed that I inspired this gaze in men old enough to be my father.

"Shame is a soul-eating emotion," Carl Jung supposedly wrote, though I can find no source for the phrase. What I know is that shame truly does gnaw at the soul, marring its goodness, its trust. My soul feels bruised, if not exactly consumed, as I work through letters, memories, coming so late to the understanding that I really understood nothing at all about men and women. I'd grown up with three brothers and I could join them and their friends for afternoons at Sooke Pot Holes or even camping trips to Bamberton Beach, and I don't think I'm wrong in remembering that there wasn't a whiff of sexual promise in the air, smoky with campfires, bright with water droplets as one after another we plunged into those icy pools in the Sooke River. But the visiting poet when I was nineteen, in his sixties by then, and breathing marriage proposals scented with whiskey; one or two others, including a man whose wife had suggested me for a scholarship and a Scottish poet with a beautiful wife, both of whom called late at night, wanting to come to my small apartment for a visit. And now not just the painter, who I knew was obsessed, "in love" he claimed, but other more trusted men were making me question my own sense of romance and friendship. Listed like this, in black and white, the shades of those men in my past make me ask myself if there was something I could have done differently. I am asking myself, the young poet I was, the one who watches me side-eyed as I come down the stairs each morning, what could I have done differently?

She looks at me, fixed for eternity by the gaze of a male painter. Or actually, she looks beyond me. But she knows I'm standing near the bottom of the stairs, hoping for a sign. What do you know about that time, I ask. What should I have done differently? You opened the envelope, she reminds me. You took those courses in Greek mythology. You knew what a pithos was. It was a jar, I remind her, not an envelope. Let's not quibble about etymology, she murmurs.

> ...the lid of the jar stopped her, by the will of
> Aegis-holding Zeus who gathers the clouds.
> But the rest, countless plagues, wander amongst
> men; for earth is full of evils and the sea is full.[53]

There were nights I walked from my apartment on Fort Street through the dark streets to the sea. What did I want, what did I hope for? That somehow everything would be as it was before I entered the gallery and saw myself, a version of myself, on a wall, wearing a hat. Was it red or was it green, and why don't I remember? I—you—were wearing a hat. From that moment, I became the object of an older man's gaze, in which he took me in, every part of my body, and put it on canvas with paints thinned with turpentine. A jar emptied of everything but hope. What did I hope for? *(Can you remember?)* His brushes were exquisite. *(Sometimes you imagined them stroking your actual skin, not what emerged from tubes of pigment—mostly red and yellow, a little blue, softened with white; but sometimes the skin was olive, sometimes lit as though from within, soft butter yellow and pink.)*

When I walked to the sea, I wanted oblivion. I wanted to pack my red backpack, as I did in May 1978, with a sleeping bag, a small blue Optimus stove, a tin plate, a mug, a fork, knife and spoon, two changes of clothing and extra shoes. I packed notebooks, my fountain pen and two boxes of ink cartridges, correction tape, paper. Packed my typewriter in a soft brown carrier. I wanted to embark on my journey to a place I'd only dreamed about, read about in poems, with a stop in London first in order to visit the Serpentine Galleries in Kensington Gardens to walk among the Henry Moore sculptures. Then a train to Holy Head, a ferry to Dublin, where I spent four days wandering streets I knew from my Irish literature courses, before taking a bus as far as Maynooth. When I got off the bus, I found the main M4 motorway west and put my thumb out. I couldn't afford any more buses or trains but somehow I was taken by kind drivers as far as I needed to go. Which was to Turlough, near Castlebar in County Mayo.

"I was seeing him about printing some drawings for me"

What I worried about:

1. that a pattern had been established and that I would never have a healthy relationship;
2. that I was truly responsible for what happened between Jack and his wife, that by opening the envelope and accepting his invitations, I had insinuated myself into the lives of others where I had no right to be;
3. that I might be giving off signals that I did not expect to be treated with respect and given appropriate space for my own work and desires;
4. that anyone could guess by just looking at me that I was not someone you should trust;
5. that 3 and 4 might be true at the same time;

6. that one day I would see a familiar figure on the sand at Eyrephort strand and that a currach would go out and bring him to the quay, that someone would point out my cottage, and that I would have nowhere to hide.

I *did* worry. How much of this is true, how much was the product of a wounded and guilty conscience, is anyone's guess. For the first two or three months of my residence on the island, I had brief conversations with people on the lane but I kept to myself. When a call came to the island's single phone, an older poet living in a nearby village inviting me to tea at his cottage in Cleggan because he'd liked a poem of mine he'd read in a literary magazine published in Dublin, I could only say no.

"I'd heard about your 'fishy' adventures from Dick Morriss," he wrote on July 26, 1978. At the time, the comment slipped away from me like a young salmon but now I read it with something approaching anger. All these years, I've thought kindly about my publisher, my editor and a few others who I believed only wished me well. But did they? Was I only ever anyone's dream girl, ready to be painted naked or seduced after a few too many drinks or taken to a little bay off Beach Avenue and made wild love to while the waves licked the sand? Because that last thing? With an older man I occasionally did some work for? I did that, allowed that, and enjoyed it. (And I don't think I regret it. He didn't. And he's long gone to spirit.) But these other men, they could dream if they chose to, but I wasn't available to them, not that way, not then nor later nor ever.

Boundary marker

bound (n.1)
c. 1300, "boundary marker," from Anglo-Latin bunda, from Old French bonde "limit, boundary, boundary stone" (12c., Modern French borne), a variant of bodne, from Medieval Latin bodina, which is perhaps from Gaulish. It is attested from mid-14c. as "an external limit, that which limits or circumscribes;" figuratively, of feelings, etc., from late 14c. From late 14c. as "limits of an estate or territory." Now chiefly in the phrase **out of bounds**, which originally referred to limits imposed on students at schools (by 1751); the other senses generally have gone with boundary.[54]

He knew no limit. No limits. No limit to his estate, to his feelings, his utterance of feelings, to what he might do with paint and pencil, no limits to what he might do with images made from a remembered moment when a young woman took off her clothes but didn't spend days in his bed or in his arms or lounging against pillows for the sake of his art. His ardour knew no limit(s).

The ancient Greeks used stones, ὅροι or *horoi*, as boundary markers. They had social meaning. Some were carved, others left undressed. They had to do with something a little different from land ownership but demarked boundaries between sacred and common ground. Who owns a girl's image? Her father? Who owns a woman's? When a man has gazed upon her body and made his mark on paper, on canvas, in the public imagination, how can a woman subvert that gaze? If she wants to, or even if she doesn't.

In the beautiful painting of a girl reaching, maybe in panic, from her white rumpled bed, to push the door of her bedroom shut, the door knob hovering almost in the centre of the composition—a boundary marker. I believe this painting was done after Jack's daughter severed her relationship with him. She was already an adult, but he was looking back, putting in place a marker that should have been there all along, the sacred ground of a girl's privacy, the common ground of the painter's eye.

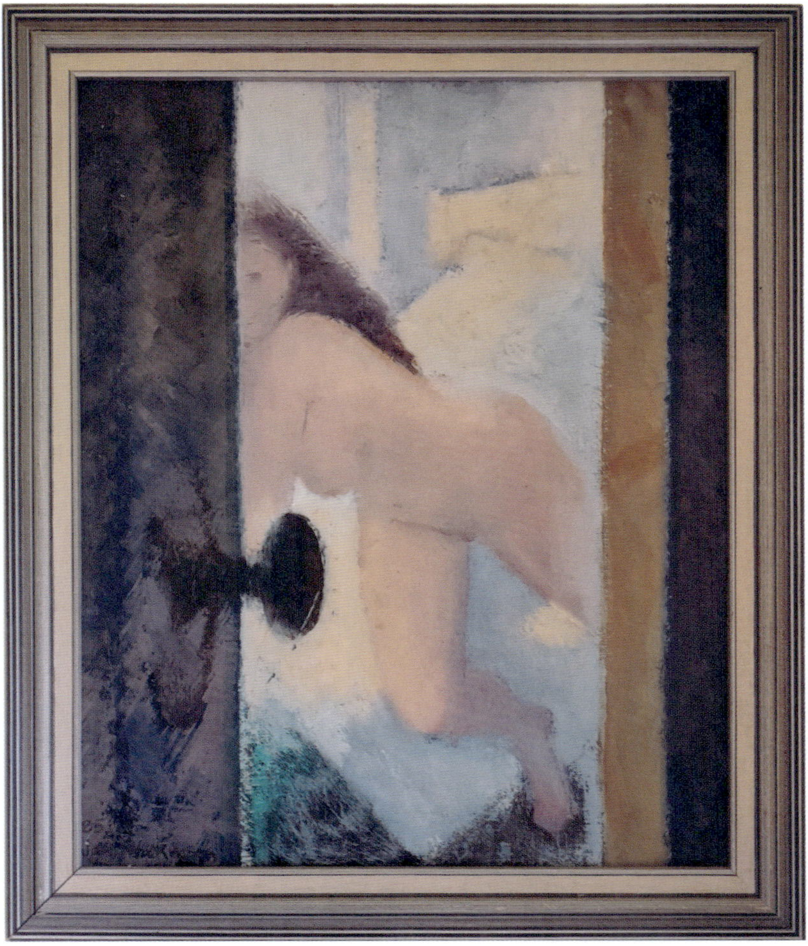

A salutation, the final regards

A painting is like a letter: they both live in the constant present. A work of fiction, say, requires the reader to follow the journey of the narrative, through all the paths and diversions that the author has laid out. The journey is grounded in the terrain of the narrative. With painting, the sudden impact of the present is conveyed as a whole, like a landscape viewed from the air. I can compare painting to a handwritten letter in the urgency to record manually what one sees and feels, but in both cases, the signing off and letting go demand fatalistic detachment. To look at a painting is to witness a first-person account of something happening *now*. The same can be said of reading a letter.[55]

I read the letters written forty-five years ago, from a painter to a muse, the muse who happened to be me. The paintings in my house are letters too—"the urgency to record manually what one sees and feels"—but in letters, the messages are carried in the complicated simplicity of words.

> You know, my dearest one, as I attempt to write down these few thoughts I'm being distracted constantly by the memory of you, last night. I don't want to cogitate about "the realities" of this existence. I only want to be with you, aye, hold you in my arms, like a man, & to hell with all of this intellectualizing of a simple, pure, honest, real love.[56]

So many letters. So much paint dried on canvas, charcoal on fine paper, a narrative of obsession, of the memory of pressure to meet, to give up my plans, to become dependent and available. A salutation, the final regards.

"Everyone carries a shadow"

Were you there too, I ask the woman with the veil of Japanese silk. Were you there with me on the beach, shadowing my walks, my quick plunges into cold water, were you waiting for me by the low fire, thirsty for creek water, a glass of smoky whiskey at dusk? Were you light, lighter than air, a goddess holding up the burden of the sky?

> Everyone carries a shadow, and the less it is embodied in the individual's conscious life, the blacker and denser it is. At all counts, it forms an unconscious snag, thwarting our most well-meant intentions.[57]

Was I with you a year or two later when you stood in the studio while he prepared his palette, were you there when I held my baby in the French restaurant and tried to shield my breast from the painter's gaze? Who was my host for the meal? Who was also the voyeur? When did I leave myself behind and when did you look away? I want to know you now, not as my shadow, but as part of my integrated self. You hang on a wall in someone's house and the only means I have to gather you in, to absorb your shadow, is to talk to you now in the photograph I have of you, your abdomen smooth and clear, not troubled by births and age.

"I'm just about ready to do some work"

> And thus the whirligig of time
> brings in his revenges.[58]

I credited him with a large spirit, essential goodness despite his obsessive pressures, yet in rereading old letters, I am horrified to discover a troubling motif that I must have read, must have noticed, but which I completely forgot.

> I'm just about ready to do some work. Don't know what will come out. I expect a lot of it will include you, my loneliness, poetry, animals, thistles, holly, pebbles, water, (surely a sea lion or two) hands (small), black lacy shawls, eyes, eyes, hooded, dark deep. (I'm not going to continue

> in this direction. It hurts.) About "nude" drawing. I'm going to make up a small folio of half a dozen and get them printed in a series of 100. By the time you get back to Victoria, if you ever do return, you will probably be quite well known, every inch of you. (May 7, 1978)

There were drawings, paintings, poses I never affected or sat for, including a large nude on a flowered cloth that went to the Art Gallery of Greater Victoria and others that went to collectors. One collector makes copies for me so I can see what he owns, my image in a house, other houses (because there are other collectors), my hair dark, tangled. My husband was given a folio of the drawings, though as it turned out, not the second folio of them, perhaps a sly nod to the old joke:

> First man: Do you have any naked pictures of your wife?
> Second man, sputtering: Of course not!
> First man: Would you like to buy some?

My husband was not offended, maybe a surprise to Jack, but looked through the folio with interest and admiration—for the artist's skill, and for the beauty of the young woman he married, because at first it seemed that these were drawings of me, not Gina. He was also given a small oil painting of an actress and writer whom Jack had known, though not as well as he'd have liked, according to the letters he wrote over the years. (He'd hoped she was interested in him, but it turned out that his daughter was the one the actress was attracted to.) She is posed like a Folies Bergère dancer, coy before the artist's gaze. I have to wonder if she'd agreed to the image or if it was produced in the same spirit as the folio of drawings of me after I'd refused Jack's attentions: "By the time you get back to Victoria, if you ever do return, you will probably be quite well known, every inch of you" (May 7, 1978). There's no question about Jack's skill. He drew constantly, his line fluent. I thought of Augustus John more than once, the ability to catch a fleeting glance, a moment of rapture, a thoughtful look on a child's face, a mother, Ida, holding her baby. The line mathematical, an equation, a complicated geometry.

I credited him with a larger spirit but reading his letters again, I realize how revenge can pull the strands of attraction and ardour into a tight knot that can never be teased free. Forty-five years later, I am holding the knot in my hands, hands he professed to love.

He drew me for years. He wrote to me for years. And then he stopped. I was older, almost a matron, and perhaps he found younger muses to occupy his imagination, his brushes, the pages of his sketchbook. I was busy, I'd returned to my own writing after a gap when my children were small, and I imagined him in one rough studio or another, the scent of turps, brushes in soup tins, his fierce gaze on someone else. I thought of him often, though I didn't go so far as to reach out. I saw the young poet in our stairwell watching me as I came down to the kitchen each morning, tiny white flowers strewn in her hair. Maybe I was closer to finally talking to her than to him. Ten years after he stopped writing the long letters

I'd find in our rural post-box, half in anticipation, half in dread, someone I know in Victoria forwarded me his obituary in the *Times Colonist*: "Jack will be remembered by his immediate and extended family, as true to himself as an Artist always."[59]

"the body turns into an axis"[60]

> By one of those optical illusions for which the architects of the restored Acropolis were renowned, the two central statues (their knees bent in mirror-image reversal) seem to carry the brunt of the roof. Its rectangular corners fall over the weight-bearing but recessive legs of their outlying sisters. Hence the roof seems to float, as if the women were supporting it by thought alone.[61]

When my husband and I were building our house, I was the mother of first one baby, and then another; by the time the second was born, the house was mostly finished, or at least finished enough to live in—it had walls, windows, plywood floors and cedar siding on its exterior. We built our house as novices, without a circle of people we could call to help with the heavy work (though my brother did come when I was pregnant with the second child to help with the trusses for a second-storey roof because otherwise I'd have to climb a high ladder into clear blue air). We'd moved far from those who might have helped. Our system was for John to frame the walls on the sixteen-by-twenty-four-foot platform that would be our kitchen, then I'd nail the plywood sheathing to the studs. We'd both lift the wall into place and I'd hold it as steady and level as I could while John nailed the floor plates down. We'd often have two-by-fours running diagonally from the tops of the walls to blocks on the floors to lift and brace the walls in place, but despite this strategy, they were heavy. I'd stand bracing the wall while John worked as quickly as he could. At a certain point, he'd need to know if the wall was level and I became adept at both holding the wall in place and sliding a level along its base and up the studs framing the sections. I didn't think of myself as strong. I was just doing the work that needed to be done. When our baby cried from the tent, waking from a nap, I'd feed him and then bring him out in his stroller or basket while we worked. Think of me, a young mother, broad-shouldered, in T-shirt and cutoff shorts, holding up the walls of a house that would become a home, a temple of sorts, a place where a family would live and grow, the house itself living and growing—we added two additions over the years to accommodate the children who arrived, those first two, and then a third, who all grew up and eventually left, returning with their own children for summers. Think of me, not a priestess of Artemis Karyatis, goddess of the nut tree, but a living column, a living support, hair in disarray, clothing not elegant veils but rags heady with creosote, cedar resins. I think of myself then and wish I'd known what I know now about strength. And beauty, which becomes richer and more durable as the years pass.

> A tug—and the wind unplaits her of braids
> and the body turns into an axis,
> while ancient light beams through her features.[62]

What I also know now is how to commemorate that process, the tall vertical studs, the horizontal lengths, not quite entablature, but top plates, lintels. In the spring of 2022, I finished the construction of the quilt top I made as a way to remember the building of our kitchen area, that first construction we did together when we began to build our house, the one we still live in forty-one years later. I wanted to remember the framing of the walls with their window spaces and openings for doors. Wanted the lintels, the places for the sills, the thresholds. I built the quilt top by sewing long strips together to serve as the studs framing the walls, I separated them with horizontal bands of beige linen to stand in for top-plates, and I used a lot of blue cotton because our plates are blue, our table linens are mostly blue, our ceiling is white, sponged with clear blue clouds, and out of every window, there is sky, some of it open and some of latticed with the Douglas firs that have grown to huge heights during our residence here. You will see some strips of brown and green. You will see some red and a coral pink,

because I couldn't "see" the finished structure as we were building it but kept asking, "Will there be window sills for geraniums, a view to roses and honeysuckle?"

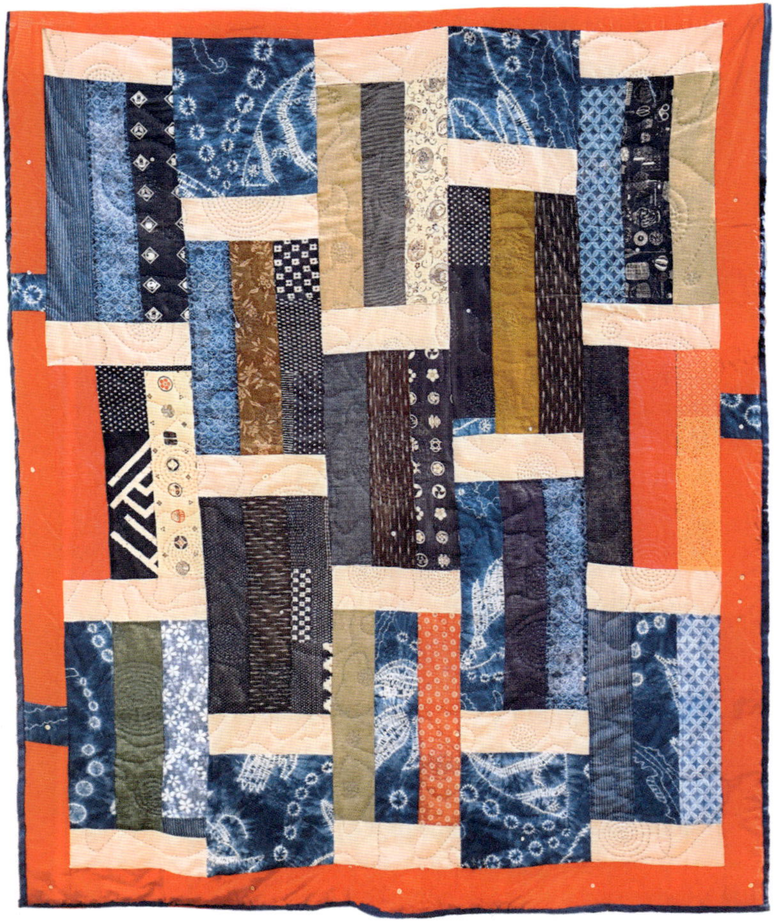

"By the time you get back to Victoria, if you ever do return, you will probably be quite well known, every inch of you"

When Jack was painting me and I was dreaming ahead to Ireland, the time ran slow. On a flowered divan, draped in a piece of silk, I thought of the work I had to do, the papers I needed to finish, the strings of my life I needed to tie up into neat bows to keep them in place. But each stroke of the brush across my flesh on the canvas, lingering on my pubis and breasts, was slow as honey. That tender yellow, the pink. The strings were too untidy to make into bows. They knotted and unravelled and I am finding tangles of them now, waiting to be teased out, smoothed, used to wrap around a stack of letters and sketches.

Now I wonder about the relationship beyond the relationship. I was young. There was no exchange of money, though he gifted me paintings worth more than any modelling session. He painted me, he desired me; I had difficulty (for whatever reason) denying him my presence. I didn't know how far he would go, that the one or two times I came to his studio and took off my clothes would result in hundreds of drawings, in poses I'd never affected; paintings of my face on a body not mine, intimacy implied that was never actual.

> The model is a prime example of this entailment: a real person who in the studio simulates an art object, Cézanne's apple, in the stillness of her posing. Whether in exchange for money or not, under gruelling conditions or not, sexually victimised or not—the model suspends her animation to present herself as to-be-seen, in service to an artist's need. In this way, she is part person, part artwork, and the artist's image of her is in part his appropriation of her and in part her recalcitrant selfhood, which he cannot or will not bend to his desire.[63]

From the other side of this gulf of years, I look back to ask questions I never knew were mine to ask. Did I simulate an art object, a naked woman holding a gauzy shawl over her head, a model, an enduring object of desire? *Take the questions into the present tense in the time that is always now.* Do I have power in this transaction? Can I say no? Can I ask that you (he) show me the images based on me? What will happen to them, where will they go? The questions that refuse the present tense. What I knew and didn't know. Didn't ask, fixed in time by his gaze.

> We are too much for ourselves—in our hungers and our desires, in our griefs and our commitments, in our loves and our hates—because we are unable to include so much of what we feel in the picture we have of ourselves. The whole idea of ourselves as excessive exposes how determined we are to have the wrong picture of what we are like, of how fanatically ignorant we are about ourselves.[64]

Years ago, when the Metropolitan Museum of Art in New York received the Balthus painting *Thérèse Dreaming* as a gift, there was uproar over its hanging. Its subject, a supposedly eleven-year-old girl (some say twelve, or fourteen), assumes a sexually suggestive pose. One writer, Wendy Steiner (also quoted above), observed, "To arrive at Balthus's image, a real girl below the age of consent had to sit in a seductive pose day after day, watched by the artist. The painting provides no insight into her thoughts or feelings on the matter. She is just a sexualised apple."[65] While I understand to some degree the feelings of others about a young girl being presented in a disturbing pose, I know something about eleven-year-old girls (I was one myself and am the mother of a young woman who was once eleven, then thirteen, and fifteen), girls on the hinge of womanhood. I know what I knew, and didn't know. I also know something about a model's experience with artists. I don't believe there is anything official to say that Thérèse ever posed in this way or that she did so day after day. That the painter saw her as a sexualized being seems to be true, but having been eleven myself, and thirteen, and fifteen, I can attest that it's not impossible that the girl was aware of herself as a potentially sexual being. This doesn't give a painter license to take advantage of that in any way. Did he, though? Did he exploit her in terms of time and consent? Was there unwanted sexual attention? That remains to be seen. Did anyone ever ask her? Did anyone ask if she'd felt like a sexualized apple? He painted her at least ten times. She was a neighbour. He also painted her brother. Did their parents know? Was she alive as the debate about the painting raged and then lingered, lingers still, in the painting world?

Jack said he fell in love with his daughter. He said he could recognize his feelings for her in the paintings he did when she would have been as young as eight. He knew his feelings were obsessive.

I wrote earlier that I didn't know how far he'd go. Now I see something in his letters and in the later paintings that troubles me. My face appears in several paintings, in poses I never sat for. I am given facial expressions that weren't or aren't mine; I wear a robe I never wore, in places I've never known. There's a folio of drawings that would have the viewer believe Jack and I shared an intense intimate relationship. I know a current societal issue is revenge porn, when an ex-lover or partner makes digital photographs and videos available to others after a breakup without the consent of the subject of the images, and how difficult it is for the woman (because 98% of people displayed on revenge porn sites are women) to have the images removed from the internet. In my case, a folio of finely reproduced drawings circulating is hardly as potentially dangerous or injurious to my reputation; neither is my image, in rich oil paint, on the walls of public galleries and in the homes of private collectors. I didn't give permission. I didn't know I could. But still. I read this again.

> About "nude" drawing. I am going to make up a small folio of half a dozen & get them printed in a series of 100. By the time you get back to Victoria, if you ever do return, you will probably be quite well known, every inch of you. (May 7, 1978)

When I first read this letter, in my cottage on the remote island off the Connemara coast, I think I was so relieved to be away from Jack that what he was saying (almost threatening, in his despair at my leaving) didn't sink in, or at least it didn't sink very deeply into my consciousness. And now, reading carefully, I have to assess our relationship, what it meant, what it didn't, all over again. That it spilled over, intentionally on his part, into the distribution of my image to collectors and galleries. I don't think I ever anticipated that.

> Now, new elements, which may give occasion for defensive measures, approach the ego from two directions—from the real external world and from the internal world of thoughts and impulses that emerge in the ego.[66]

Reading the stack of letters, revisiting the notebooks and ephemera he gave to me, I have to wonder why I am troubled now, so far away in years and geography, in need of Freud's defensive measures. The impulse that emerges in my particular ego is to move on, with gratitude for the portraits and sketches of a younger self at the heart of who I am, even if I forget her most days. Jack sketched and painted me in love, in anger, out of obsessive feelings, even as an act of mild revenge, though I don't believe he began with that specific intention, that resonance. I may have served as a muse but his gaze in my direction was indirectly in service to the intended audience of the work, the men who shared news of me with one another and might just like to own the drawings in their neat brown folder.

> By the way, I promised Robin a drawing of you, sometime. Robin & I, in our cups, got around to promising to exchange works.[67]

Robin, who thought that maybe one of these drawings could be used on the cover of my forthcoming book? (As inexperienced as I was as a young writer, susceptible to both praise and rejection, I knew *that* was not a good idea.) What they saw in the drawings might have surprised them. The implied intimacy, the dishevelled bed, body fully displayed. Is this the only way they saw me, a work to be exchanged, chortled over, shared? Of course not. One of them was my cherished mentor. But I suspect he was also first in the line for the folio of drawings. ("I promised Robin a drawing of you.") Another owned the publishing company responsible for my second book. When I was in dire financial straits, he gave me work for a week organizing a book collection and archives, paying me generously. Another sent editing work my way and employed me when he could in a bookstore. But now, reading the lines, reading between the lines, I find another narrative; even from this distance of forty-five years, I am embarrassed, uncomfortable with their attention, even though all of them are dead. The gaze, on behalf of them and others, wasn't something I was aware of then, but now I can't forget it. The portrait of me as a young poet with flowers in my hair is watching him watching me. We are left, the young poet, the young mother with her baby, the girl reaching to push the door shut, the elegant cool woman in the red robe, the actress as Folies Bergère girl, and they are gone, the ones who had access to us because of paint and brush, the intricacies of copy machines. We shake away the gaze like an insect's wings too close, too close, and we look at our younger selves, look them directly in the eyes, the averted eyes (turn, turn), claiming our own bodies again, our faces.

"Always"

> I don't want to seem abnormal to you. I am not that quaint, only profoundly in love. Such extremes of feeling have been known to make the coolest, most level-headed, seem to behave like madmen. Many, many times, I've asked myself what it is that I want, really. The nearest I can come to it is, dearest Theresa, that I want to be near you, always. (May 1, 1978)

I am shaking off the words that followed me from Victoria to Ireland, from a moment when I could have made a bigger mistake than the one I made when I opened the letter, let myself be flattered as he drew my face.

A line here, and here, and here

My friend, visiting from the Netherlands, carries a ladder into the stairwell to lift the portrait of the young poet down from its hook. I have looked at it for decades, my younger self behind glass, a few white flowers strewn in my hair. We carry the painting to the long pine table and I brush the winter's dust off the frame. My friend, an artist, tells me the work was done on canvas board. He shows me how the ground would have been prepared—dark, on the white board—and how the outline of the head (my head) was sketched with a few dark brushstrokes. He follows the line. We talk about the mechanics of making a work like this one. Colour from a tube, the brushes, the places where the pigment is thick because perhaps the brush was dirty and he scuffed off the paint. Probably done in one session, my friend says. The strokes are quick. We look at the eyes (my eyes), the nose, the blue of the waistcoat, strokes of the same colour along the right shoulder. The hair he thinks was black with some blue. "Shall we take it out of its frame?" he asks. Who knows what we might find behind the backing.

The backing is cardboard, taped together with masking tape. There is an inscription on the back, wishing the recipient (my daughter) a happy life. Tiny nails hold the cardboard against the frame; my friend removes them with needle-nose pliers. We lift away the back and the same inscription is written across the underside of the canvas board. It was so long ago: June 15, 1993. My daughter would have been nearly eight years old, the same age as Gina in her ballet leotard in one of my favourite paintings of her.

In the day's clear light, my hair is not black and blue but deep burgundy. From the distance of the stairs below, my hair was lustrous, my skin smooth, but close up, I can see some of the oil has separated from the pigment and shows as a smear, spackled with faint white lines. My mouth is lovely. My friend shows me how the flowers in my hair might have been an afterthought, a way to use up some white paint on a brush that has limned the deep V of my neck. He suspects the painter was thrifty with his materials.

I see the haste of this work, the urge to put the young poet down on canvas, the firm line of the right part of my head. I see how he would have sketched with a brush dipped in black, a line here, and here, and here. My friend shows how the eyes are not symmetrical and they are the eyes I see in the mirror every day, not symmetrical, but these are not looking at me, not directly; they are implicating me in something I am only now discovering.

A day later, this morning, I come down the stairs early and look up to the blank wall. A small hook to hold the wire at the back of the frame, which has been dismantled, the painting resting flat in a safe place. Everything has been taken apart, dusted, looked at closely. I have talked and talked and talked. A blank wall, and somehow I don't know where to look, whose eyes to meet. A line here, and here, and here, and on the face I see in the mirror, a line here, and here, and here.

"But the woman took off the great lid of the jar with her hands"

On a holiday in Greece in 1932, Virginia Woolf met her younger self:

> Yes, but what can I say about the Parthenon—that my own ghost met me, the girl of 23, with all her life to come…[68]

I was twenty when the stalker phoned my mother repeatedly, twenty-one when I climbed those marble steps to the Parthenon, twenty-three when I met Jack Wilkinson. My life was also to come and I am alive now, alive as I sort letters and sketches, the rooms of my house filled with women, ghosts if you like: who I was, who Jack hoped I would be, who I became in the fullness of time.

When I held up the raw walls of my kitchen, when I cradled my baby in the night in a chilly tent, wrapping him in a blanket my mother had crocheted, when I pushed a wheelbarrow full of sand to be mixed with cement and water to become the footings of our house, I was using my body in its strength and purpose, the width of my shoulders an entablature of my life to come. I removed the cap from a five-gallon receptacle and lowered it into the lake for water because we didn't yet have a well, let the container fill, bracing my legs in the soft earth at the shore as I lifted it to bring it back to the work site, a little water splashing on my feet. Before that, I was the large young woman among slender ones; before that, a girl who didn't fit in with her peers and who read novels and poetry to stay alive in all her senses. Who lunched with Frank and couldn't say no. After I held up the walls, I brushed my hands on my pants and went on to the next chore. I forgot for a time what I was capable of. The writing I loved and that had sustained my heart and mind in my twenties left me. It no longer found the fertile ground in my imagination. Like seeds that need fire to germinate, it stayed dormant, waiting, waiting, as the years passed. Then I was myself the fire. Essays, novels, novellas, a memoir and more, more, the words unspooling like the threads I was also using to stitch quilts. I burned with intention, with energy.

We raised another heavy beam to replace the original one across our patio. It held wisteria from John's grandmother's plant in Suffolk, a root of it brought back by John's mother in her suitcase. We gently laid the vine on its side over sawhorses while the new beam, sawn from cedar cut on our own land, rested on posts and blocks. "Can you hold it in place?" John asked, and yes, like one of the Erectheion Kore, I could. I did. When the beam was securely fastened with long spikes, we coaxed the vine around its new supports. It ranges along the beam, its wood twisted and elegant. Years later it blooms spectacularly, cascades of mauve blossoms hanging over us as we carry groceries across the patio. On early summer nights I smell it from my bed, a living entablature of air and growth. It is a haven for bees and hummingbirds, the quick rush of weasels in pursuit of mice.

Mornings, I paused by the poet with flowers in her hair, and will pause again once she has been given a new frame. "What do you have to tell me?" I'll ask. That same old question.

> But the woman took off the great lid of the
> jar with her hands and scattered all these
> and her thought caused sorrow and mischief
> to men. Only Hope remained there in an
> unbreakable home within under the rim of the
> great jar, and did not fly out at the door...[69]

Pandora, the holder of the pithos, was herself a gift. Her name tells us that: Πανδώρα, the all-gifted, giver of all, though it's hard to think of the contents of her vessel as welcome. So many in this story have died. So many I no longer know, including Sheryl and Meg, whom I haven't seen in decades. Do I have hope? For anyone? I do, for myself most of all. The Karyatids once held phiales in one hand, shallow vessels for drinking or gifts, or for pouring libations for others. They take the weight of the entablature on their bodies, their legs tensed, their hair arranged to detract from the strain on their necks, their hands reaching forward. Before Leonardo, their creator knew the motion of the surface of the water, knew the flow of the surface, the lines of the eddies. Can you imagine such strength, such purpose?

In the British Museum, where the lost Karyatid languishes, dreaming of her sisters and the temple of her origins, there is a phiale from roughly the same period as the maidens: the fifth century BCE. It was broken and has been pieced together, its omphalos black and yellow circles, surrounded by spirals, and around the spirals, decorations depicting a hunt—four hounds and a huntsman chasing a hare—and surrounding that, crows, foxes, scorpions and snakes. I imagine one of the Kore holding it, delighted to be offering a libation in such a beautiful ritual vessel, form and function so artfully combined. That was before the cannon-fire, the theft, the smog of the city below, the damage. What we consider a curse can also be a gift. I opened an envelope containing a naked drawing and an invitation. Reading the subsequent letters of love and obsession written to me decades ago, when I was young and beautiful, though hardly aware of the latter, reminds me of how much pain I caused Jack, his wife, possibly his children, and also how much anxiety and hurt he caused me. How much shame. When you are offered a gift, it comes with words of caution, or at least it should. It should come with hope, but what would that look like? What could I have told him then, or what could he have told me that would have smoothed the sadness, the anger? I was too young to know the words.

Turn to me, I tell all the young women in my house, the ones who are me, the ones who are resemblances, archetypes, versions. The one who isn't. And the other one, too. Turn to me. On my walls you are beautiful, as you were then and still are, burnished by time's soft-edged brush. There is so much in your future and I am waiting for you, waiting for you to turn and remember me, as I remember you.

Turn, I will ask the young poet with flowers in her hair, you who have kept a certain privacy for decades, watching me descend the stairs, you who also watched me climb them, weary or joyous or lost in thought. I carried sorrow up the stairs and down them too. I felt your gaze in the ascent and the descent. Watch me. Watch me open my hands, releasing the shame I carried, hidden mostly but always a weight, an unnecessary guilt. I took off my clothes and I am commemorated with Cadmium Yellow lightened with Flake White, Alizarin Crimson, Prussian Blue, Viridian, Chrome Green. The warm light shimmering with Titanium Buff, Yellow Ochre. My hair, Thalo Blue, Thalo Green, Alizarin Crimson, Indian Yellow, underlayered with transparent yellow. On the Irish island, I walked on the rocks in grey mist and wrapped my arms around my body to contain myself. "Let a body venture at last."[70] At last I am at least unwrapping the veil, shaking the words from its fine gauze. What happens next, happens. There is no one now to hold me in that fierce gaze, as dangerous as it was loving.

Acknowledgements

I am grateful to the people who helped me locate materials or who offered advice, who answered questions and who simply listened as I worked out my own feelings about writing this memoir:

- Heather Dean, Associate Director, Special Collections, at the University of Victoria, for kindly scanning the pages of a notebook in my fonds in the Collections;
- Christina Johnson-Dean, for offering an art historian's perspective;
- Walter van Broekhuizen, for patiently describing the methods and materials relevant to one of the paintings discussed in these pages;
- Forrest Pass, my older son, for convincing me not to burn the letters at the heart of this work and for talking to me about archives in general and my own in particular;
- Fraser McColl, for his generous correspondence and willingness to allow access to his art collection;
- and my husband John Pass, for our years together, and for understanding the weight of this story in my life.

I am also grateful to the team at Thornapple Press for their excellent care and attention to this book. Eve Rickert guided the process, Hazel Boydell kept us all in touch, Andrea Zanin was a careful and intelligent editor, and Heather van der Hoop brought a keen eye to the copyediting, asking good questions. Thanks to Jeff Werner, for the type design and his artist's eye, and to Naomi MacDougall and Jessica Sullivan, for the most beautiful cover ever. I'd also like to thank Chelsea Roisum for her photographic skill and lively spirit.

Source Materials

As well as the Jack Wilkinson paintings that hang on the walls of the house I built with my husband John Pass, I relied on personal correspondence between Jack and me, beginning in March 1978 and concluding in 1997. Jack also presented me with a hardbound volume of more formal letters he wrote in May 1978, which he titled *Five Letters to Theresa*." And because he was encouraging me to make art myself, he gave me a small sketchbook he labelled "Notes on Painting (for Theresa)," in which he explained how to prepare materials, how to fill a canvas, etc.; the notes quickly became obsessive sketches of me and expressions of his affection. In 1981, he sent me a long essay entitled "My Life for Theresa Kishkan," a detailed biographical (and often psychological) self-portrait. I also consulted my own journals, though I was never faithful about keeping them..

Memory is a great archive and a consolation. I've tried to be as true as I was able to be, recognizing that time has a way of smoothing and refining the way I think about the past. My stories overlap the stories of others, both friends and acquaintances, the living and the dead; my intention was never to hurt anyone but to understand what happened nearly five decades ago, and how events shaped and affected relationships. Other people may remember this time differently. I've changed the names of some of the individuals in this memoir, but others, who then and now have a more public presence, remain themselves.

Catalogue Raissoné

p. viii Jack Wilkinson, "Young Poet," 1982, oil on canvas board, 17.5 × 23.5 inches, owned by Angelica Pass.

p. 18 Jack Wilkinson, untitled sketch, ink on paper, 1978, 4 × 6 inches, from a notebook owned by Theresa Kishkan.

p. 26 Collage using primary materials. Photograph by Chelsea Roisum.

p. 55 Karyatids, Photo by Wknight94 (Wikimedia Commons, CC BY-SA 3.0 https://creativecommons.org/licenses/by-sa/3.0/).

p. 60 Jack Wilkinson, untitled, no date, oil on canvas board, 30 × 36 inches, owned by Fraser McColl.

p. 109 Jack Wilkinson, untitled (woman and baby), 1982, oil on stretched canvas, 24 × 36 inches, owned by Theresa Kishkan.

p. 132 Theresa Kishkan, untitled (Irish cottage), 1978, oil on canvas paper, 12 × 15.5 inches, owned by Theresa Kishkan.

p. 134 Jack Wilkinson, untitled sketch (woman and child), 1990, reproduction of ink on paper (made by artist due to rapid deterioration of paper), 9 × 13 inches, owned by Theresa Kishkan.

p. 142 Jack Wilkinson, "Girl in a Red Robe," 1982, canvas board, 21.5 × 26.5 inches, owned by Brendan Pass.

p. 157 Jack Wilkinson, "Morning Nude," 1991, oil on canvas board, 19 × 23.5 inches, owned by Theresa Kishkan and John Pass.

p. 170 Theresa Kishkan, untitled quilt, 2022, cotton, linen, hand-dyed indigo, akoya shell, 76 × 91 inches, owned by Theresa Kishkan.

Notes

1 Hesiod, "Works and Days," *The Homeric Hymns and Homerica*, translated by H. G. Evelyn-White, Perseus Digital Library, https://www.perseus.tufts.edu/hopper/text?doc=urn:cts:greekLit:tlg0020.tlg002.perseus-eng1:83-108.

2 Jack Wilkinson, *Five Letters to Theresa*.

3 Jacques Lacan, Écrits, translated by Bruce Fink (W. W. Norton and Company, 2006), https://mforbes.sites.getty.

4 Milan Kundera, *The Book of Laughter and Forgetting*, translated by Michael Henry Heim (Knopf, 1980), 285.

5 Kundera, *The Book of Laughter and Forgetting*, 285.

6 Manuela Ammer, "Where Does a Sculpture Start and Where Does It End?" *Frieze*, August 11, 2011, https://www.frieze.com/article/where-does-sculpture-start-and-where-does-it-end.

7 Wilkinson, *Five Letters.*

8 Theresa Kishkan, "Olea Europeana: Young Woman with Eros on her Shoulder," in *Mnemonic: A Book of Trees* (Goose Lane Editions, 2011).

9 Sigmund Freud to Romain Rolland, in *The Standard Edition of the Complete Psychological Works of Sigmund Freud*, translated by James Strachey, in collaboration with Anna Freud, volume 22 (1932–36), (Hogarth Press and the Institute of Psycho-Analysis, 1964), 246.

10 Julia Kristeva, "Stabat Mater," in *The Kristeva Reader*, edited by Toril Moi (Columbia University Press, 1986), 162.

11 Kundera, *The Book of Laughter and Forgetting*, 285.

12 John Berger, *Ways of Seeing* (Penguin Classic, 2008), 54.

13 Kristeva, "Stabat Mater," 162.

14 C. G. Jung, *Visions: Notes of the Seminar Given in 1930–1934*, edited by Claire Douglas (Routledge, 1998).

15 Berger, *Ways of Seeing*, 54.

16 W. B. Yeats, "Leda and the Swan," https://poets.org/poem/leda-and-swan.

17 Kristeva, "Stabat Mater," 162.

18 Wilkinson, "My Life for Theresa Kishkan," unpublished essay, 1981.

19 Annette Kämmerer, "The Scientific Underpinnings and Impacts of Shame," *Scientific American*, August 9, 2019, https://www.scientificamerican.com/article/the-scientific-underpinnings-and-impacts-of-shame/.

20 Kämmerer, "The Scientific Underpinnings and Impacts of Shame."

21 Jung, *Part I: Archetypes and the Collective Unconscious*, volume 9, edited and translated by G. Adler and R. F. C. Hull (Princeton University Press, 1980), https://www.jungiananalysts.org.uk/wp-content/uploads/2018/07/C.-G.-Jung-Collected-Works-Volume-9i_-The-Archetypes-of-the-Collective-Unconscious.pdf, 42.

22 Freud to Rolland, in *Complete Psychological Works*, 246.

23 Brian D. Johnson, "Atom's Journey," *Maclean's*, September 13, 1999, https://reader.macleans.ca/macleans/19990913/index.html#p64.

24 Johnson, "Atom's Journey."

25 Now as I proofread the pages of this book, I've found an interview with Atom Egoyan published in March 2025, in which the interviewer notes: "…he revealed that as a teenager in Victoria, B.C., he fell in love with a young woman who was engaged in an incestuous romance with her father, a respected artist. The woman, later identified as Gina Wilkinson, became an actor, playwright and director. She died in 2010." https://zoomer.com/the-z-list/2025/03/06/sex-lies-and-opera-director

-atom-egoyan-talks-commuting-between-stage-and-screen -and-the-personal-trauma-behind-seven-veils.

26 Amanda Campbell, "Gina Wilkinson: I Can Feel Her Glimmer," *The Way I See It Theatre and Music Blog*, January 25, 2011, https://www.twisitheatreblog.com/?p=563.

27 Celia Paul, *Letters to Gwen John* (New York Review Books, 2022), 233–34.

28 Freud to Rolland, in *Complete Psychological Works*, 246.

29 Camille Paglia, *Glittering Images: A Journey Through Art From Egypt to Star Wars* (Pantheon Books, 2012), 24.

30 Kämmerer, "The Scientific Underpinnings and Impacts of Shame."

31 Kristeva, "Stabat Mater," 174.

32 Wilkinson, "My Life for Theresa Kishkan."

33 Kristeva, "Stabat Mater," 166.

34 Lacan, "Logical Time and the Assertion of Anticipated Certainty: A New Sophism," in *Newsletter of the Freudian Field* 2, no. 2: 12.

35 Freud, "A Disturbance of Memory on the Acropolis," in *The Standard Edition of the Complete Psychological Works of Sigmund Freud*, vol. xxii (1932–36), translated by James Strachey, in collaboration with Anna Freud (Hogarth Press and the Institute of Psycho-Analysis, 1964), 246.

36 Wilkinson, *Five Letters*, footnote.

37 Freud to Rolland in *Complete Psychological Works*, 246.

38 Wilkinson, *Five Letters.*

39 Paul, *Self-Portrait* (Jonathan Cape, 2019), 96–97.

40 Wilkinson, *Five Letters.*

41 Kämmerer, "The Scientific Underpinnings and Impacts of Shame."

42 Kämmerer, "The Scientific Underpinnings and Impacts of Shame."

43 Wilkinson, *Five Letters.*

44 Mark Norton, "Alienation of Affection," *Infinity Law*, November 16, 2019, https://www.infinity-law.com/post/alienation-of-affections-a-wife-cheated-the-husband-sued-he-won.

45 Leonardo da Vinci, *The Complete Notebooks of Leonardo da Vinci*, translated by Jean Paul Richter (1888), https://zelalemkibret.files.wordpress.com/2012/02/the-complete-works-leonardo-da-vinci.pdf.

46 Yeats, "Leda and the Swan," https://www.poetryfoundation.org/poems/43292/leda-and-the-swan.

47 Yeats, "Leda and the Swan."

48 Wilkinson, *Five Letters.*

49 Kristeva, "Stabat Mater," 162.

50 Hermann Minkowski, "Space and Time," Address to the 80th Meeting of the Natural Scientists, Cologne, September 21, 1908, in *Space and Time: Minkowski's Papers on Relativity*, translated by F. Lewertoff and V. Petkov, edited by V. Petkov (Minkowski Institute Press, 2012), https://mathweb.ucsd.edu/~b3tran/cgm/Minkowski_SpaceAndTime_1909.pdf.

51 Wilkinson, "My Life for Theresa Kishkan."

52 Freud, "Infantile Sexuality," *Three Essays on the Theory of Sexuality,* translated by James Strachey (Avon Books, 1965), 175.

53 Hesiod, "Works and Days," *The Homeric Hymns and Homerica.*

54 Etymonline, "Bound," https://www.etymonline.com/word/Bound.

55 Paul, "Notes on Craft," *Granta*, April 7, 2022, https://granta.com/notes-on-craft-celia-paul/.

56 Wilkinson, *Five Letters.*

57 Jung, *Psychology and Religion* (Yale University Press, 1938), 131.

58 William Shakespeare, *Twelfth Night*, Act 5, scene 1, 377.

59 "John Wilkinson Obituary," *Times Colonist*, September 2, 2007, https://www.legacy.com/ca/obituaries/timescolonist/name/john-wilkinson-obituary?id=46163830.

60 Halyna Petrosanyak, "The Caryatid," translated by Michael M. Naydan, https://www.poetryinternational.com/en/poets-poems/poems/poem/103-8227_THE-CARYATID/.
61 Paglia, "*Glittering Images*," 24.
62 Halyna Petrosanyak, "The Caryatid."
63 Wendy Steiner, "Artists' Models Are Real People – We Mustn't Forget This When We Look at Art," Apollo, February 14, 2018, https://www.apollo-magazine.com/artists-models-are-real-people-we-mustnt-forget-this-when-we-look-at-art/.
64 Adam Phillips, *On Balance* (Penguin, 2011), 35.
65 Steiner, "Artists' Models Are Real People."
66 Freud, "A Disturbance of Memory on the Acropolis," 245.
67 Wilkinson, *Five Letters*.
68 Virginia Woolf, *The Diary of Virginia Woolf*, volume IV (1931–35), edited by Anne Olivier Bell (The Hogarth Press, 1982), April 1932, 90.
69 Hesiod, "Works and Days," *The Homeric Hymns and Homerica*.
70 Kristeva, "Stabat Mater," 162.

Bibliography

Ammer, Manuela. "Where Does a Sculpture Start and Where Does It End?" *Frieze*, August 11, 2011. https://www.frieze.com/article/where-does-sculpture-start-and-where-does-it-end.

Balthus, as dictated to *Alain Vircondelet. Vanished Splendors: A Memoir*, trans. Benjamin Ivry. Ecco Press, 2002.

Berger, John. *Ways of Seeing*. Penguin Classic, 2008.

Bovey, Patricia. *A Passion for Art: The Art and Dynamics of the Limners*. Sono Nis Press, 1996.

Campbell, Amanda. "Gina Wilkinson: I Can Feel Her Glimmer," *The Way I See It Theatre and Music Blog*, January 25, 2011, https://www.twisitheatreblog.com/?p=563.

da Vinci, Leonardo. *The Complete Notebooks of Leonardo da Vinci*, translated by Jean Paul Richter (1888), https://zelalemkibret.files.wordpress.com/2012/02/the-complete-works-leonardo-da-vinci.pdf.

Etymonline, "Bound," https://www.etymonline.com/word/Bound.

Freud, Sigmund. *The Standard Edition of the Complete Psychological Works of Sigmund Freud*, translated by James Strachey, in collaboration with Anna Freud. Volume xxii (1932-36). Hogarth Press and the Institute of Psycho-Analysis, 1964).

Hesiod. "Works and Days." In *The Homeric Hymns and Homerica*. Translated by H. G. Evelyn-White. Perseus Digital Library. https://www.perseus.tufts.edu/hopper/text?doc=urn:cts:greekLit:tlg0020.tlg002.perseus-eng1:83-108.

"John Wilkinson Obituary," *Times Colonist*, September 2, 2007, https://www.legacy.com/ca/obituaries/timescolonist/name/john-wilkinson-obituary?id=46163830.

Johnson, Brian D. "Atom's Journey," *Maclean's*, September 13, 1999, https://reader.macleans.ca/macleans/19990913/index.html#p64.

Jung, Carl. *The Archetypes and the Collective Unconscious*, 2nd ed., translated by R.F.C. Hull, edited by H. Read, M. Fordham and G. Adler. Princeton University Press, 1968.

Jung, Carl. *Visions: Notes of the Seminar Given in 1930–1934*, edited by Claire Douglas (Routledge, 1998).

Kämmerer, Annette. "The Scientific Underpinnings and Impacts of Shame," *Scientific American*, August 9, 2019, https://www.scientificamerican.com/article/the-scientific-underpinnings-and-impacts-of-shame/.

Kishkan, Theresa. *Mnemonic: A Book of Trees*. Goose Lane Editions, 2011.

Kristeva, Julia. *The Kristeva Reader*, translated by Léon S. Roudiez and Seán Hand, edited by Toril Moi. Columbia University Press, 1986.

Kundera, Milan. *The Book of Laughter and Forgetting*, trans. Aaron Asher. Harper Modern Classics, 1999.

Lacan, Jacques. Écrits, trans. Bruce Fink. W. W. Norton and Company, 2006. https://mforbes.sites.gettysburg.edu/cims226/wp-content/uploads/2018/09/Week-4a-Jacques-Lacan.pdf.

Lacan, Jacques. "Logical Time and the Assertion of Anticipated Certainty: A New Sophism," in *Newsletter of the Freudian Field*. Fall, 1988, 2, no. 2: 12.

Minkowski, Hermann. "Space and Time," Address to the 80th Meeting of the Natural Scientists, Cologne, September 21, 1908, in *Space and Time: Minkowski's Papers on Relativity*, translated by F. Lewertoff and V. Petkov, edited by V. Petkov. Minkowski Institute Press, 2012. https://mathweb.ucsd.edu/~b3tran/cgm/Minkowski_SpaceAndTime_1909.pdf.

Norton, Mark. "Alienation of Affection." *Infinity Law*. November 16, 2019. https://www.infinity-law.com/post/alienation-of-affections-a-wife-cheated-the-husband-sued-he-won.

Paglia, Camille. *Glittering Images: A Journey Through Art From Egypt to Star Wars*. Pantheon Books, 2012.

Paul, Celia. *Self-Portrait*. Jonathan Cape, 2019.

Paul, Celia. *Letters to Gwen John*. NYRB, 2022.

Paul, Celia. "Notes on Craft." *Granta*. April 7, 2022. https://granta.com/notes-on-craft-celia-paul/.

Petrosanyak, Halyna. "The Caryatid," trans. Michael M. Naydan. https://www.poetryinternational.com/en/poets-poems/poems/poem/103-8227_THE-CARYATID/.

Phillips, Adam. *On Balance*. Penguin Books, 2011.

Shakespeare, William. *Twelfth Night*.

Steiner, Wendy. "Artists' Models Are Real People – We Mustn't Forget This When We Look at Art." *Apollo*. February 14, 2018. https://www.apollo-magazine.com/artists-models-are-real-people-we-mustnt-forget-this-when-we-look-at-art/.

Woolf, Virginia. *The Diary of Virginia Woolf, Volume IV, 1931-35*, ed. Anne Olivier Bell. The Hogarth Press, 1982.

Yeats, W. B. "Leda and the Swan." https://poets.org/poem/leda-and-swan.

Also from Thornapple Press

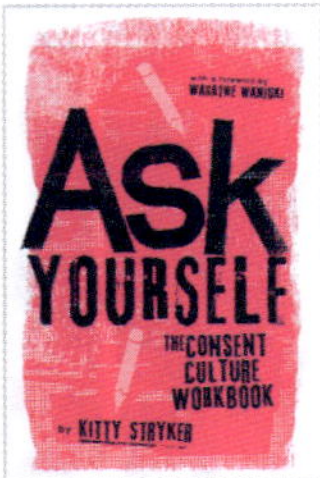

Ask Yourself: The Consent Culture Workbook

Kitty Stryker

"Kitty Stryker invites readers to delve deeper, with guest experts and personal anecdotes, to manifest a culture of consent in one's own community that starts at the heart."

—Jiz Lee, editor of *Coming Out Like a Porn Star*

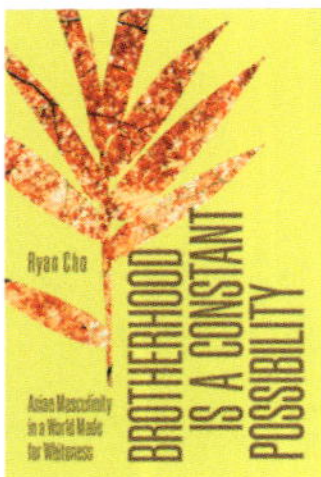

Brotherhood is a Constant Possibility: Asian Masculinity in a World Made for Whiteness

Ryan Cho

A deeply personal, provocative portrait of how race, culture and sexuality intersect to reshape what it means to be an Asian man in North America today.

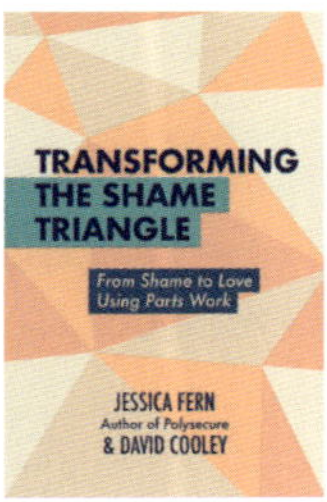

Transforming the Shame Triangle: From Shame to Love Using Parts Work

Jessica Fern and David Cooley

"A fresh, insightful take on one of our slipperiest emotions that offers readers workable pathways forward."

—*Kirkus Reviews*

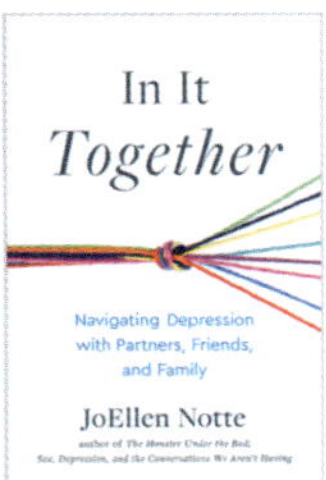

In It Together: Navigating Depression with Partners, Friends, and Family

JoEllen Notte

"A must-have resource for anyone experiencing depression and for the people who love someone struggling with depression."

—Jessica Fern, author of *Polysecure: Attachment, Trauma and Consensual Nonmonogamy*

Theresa Kishkan lives on the Sechelt Peninsula, BC with her husband, poet John Pass. She has published 16 books, including *Euclid's Orchard*, a collection of essays about family history, botany, mathematics and love (Mother Tongue Publishing, 2017); a novella, *The Weight of the Heart* (Palimpsest Press, 2020); and *Blue Portugal and Other Essays* (University of Alberta Press, 2022), a collection of lyrical essays. Her books have been nominated for many awards, including the Hubert Evans Award and the Ethel Wilson Prize. Theresa's essay collection *Phantom Limb* received the inaugural Readers' Choice Award from the Creative Nonfiction Collective in 2008.

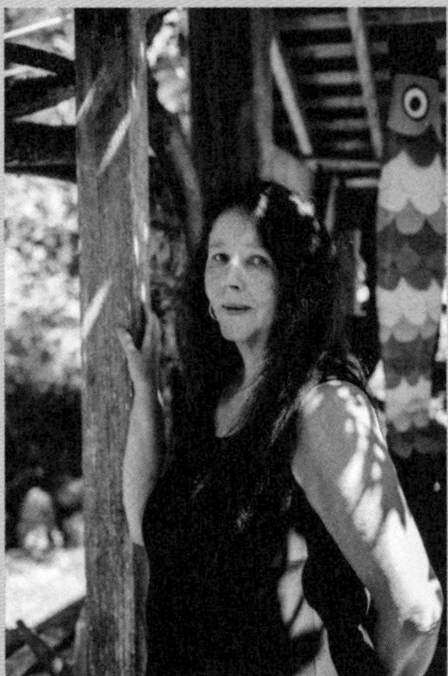